UNDERSTANDING
STATISTICAL METHODS

UNDERSTANDING STATISTICAL METHODS

A Manual for Students and Data Analysts

Chester H. McCall

Writers Club Press
San Jose New York Lincoln Shanghai

Understanding Statistical Methods
A Manual for Students and Data Analysts

Writers Club Press
an imprint of iUniverse, Inc.

For information address:
iUniverse, Inc.
5220 S. 16th St., Suite 200
Lincoln, NE 68512
www.iuniverse.com

ISBN: 1-58348-841-3

Printed in the United States of America

CONTENTS

LIST OF EXHIBITS

CHAPTER 4

CHAPTER 5

CHAPTER 6

PREFACE

This manual represents the culmination of almost 40 years of teaching and applying statistical methods to real-world problems and issues.

In 1952, while a graduate student at The George Washington University in Washington, D.C., I was "inserted" into an introductory statistics course, as instructor, for students taking psychology, sociology, or education degrees, ranging from the bachelor to the doctoral level. "Inserted" is a really descriptive word since the faculty member who was scheduled to teach the course resigned the day before the course was to be offered. Hence, I adjusted to moving from a planned graduate assistant role in a statistics lab to an instructor in a basic statistics course for the first time. To say the least, this first teaching experience was stressful, difficult, and at best modestly rewarding. But, learning from my errors and experience, I made an effort to convert the detailed derivations and endless equations to a format that would make the subject somewhat palatable to students. Unfortunately, while the objective was commendable, the implementation was not the best.

Seven years later, I entered the consulting profession and served solely in that capacity for 23 years. In 1982 I returned to the teaching profession, being fortunate enough to secure a position as an Associate Professor at the Graduate School of Education and Psychology, Pepperdine University in the Los Angeles area.

Teaching the first class in the fall of 1982 to students in the Ed.D. program in Institutional Management convinced me that times had not really changed much. Textbooks were still using classical approaches (even my introductory text published by Iowa State University Press). Students still had the attitude that, if they waited long enough, statistics, as a requirement, would vanish from the curriculum and all would be well. Such was not the case and never will be. An understanding of statistical methods is critical to good research, management, and just plain analysis of problems and issues that develop within our society.

So, as we entered the information technology age and Pepperdine moved from having two small personal computer systems to having many electronic classrooms and personal computers in virtually all offices, it became apparent to me that the classical approach was not working and would not work. It was time for a change.

This manual is the result of my teaching and consulting experiences, as well as my personal introduction in 1984 to the value of the personal computer as a tool. Now I am "hooked" on personal computers and feel that an understanding of this technology, as a tool, is critical in virtually all professions. Why not in teaching and understanding statistics?

This text has been written to follow, as closely as possible, my personal teaching style, which is aimed at eliminating fear of the subject while making the concepts clear. It is my hope that this desire on my part has been accomplished.

I am indebted to many individuals and organizations for their support in this effort: to the Research Division of the National Education Association for its initial encouragement in preparing the introductory text in statistics for people in the field of education; to Pepperdine University for supporting a sabbatical which, in part, has led to this manual; to Dr. Gabriella Belli, Associate Professor at Virginia Polytechnic Institute, for her cooperation in initiating research on teaching statistics to adult graduate students who work full-time while pursuing their advanced degrees in the evenings and on weekends; to Drs. Kathy Green and Jack Anderson for their in-depth review of this document and the valuable suggestions which they have made; to Teri Greene, a doctoral student at Pepperdine, for her detailed review of this manual from a student's perspective; to my wife Linda whose published works are far more exciting and interesting than mine, for her understanding that time has been essential to completing this manual, and to her perceptive editorial review of several drafts of this manual; and, to the dozens of students, both at The George Washington University and Pepperdine University, Graduate School of Education and Psychology, who through their patience in sitting through statistics and their comments and review of the various versions of this manual.

And, finally, to my Christian friends who throughout this process have prayed that what resulted would bring credit to our Lord, I give thanks.

1. INTRODUCTION

This chapter presents a background discussion and describes the purpose of this manual. In addition some basic concepts are presented. *Any word or phrase which is followed by an * the first time it occurs in the text and is also underlined appears in the Glossary at the end of this manual.*

Background and Purpose of Manual

Statistics, sometimes referred to as "sadistics," can be viewed from many perspectives. Unfortunately, most of them carry a negative connotation. I even felt this way about the subject when first exposed to it many years ago. However, being blessed with an excellent teacher and having had a curiosity about the subject, I developed a deep conviction that statistics is a tool which can serve many professions and address problems, issues, and dilemmas of concern to all of us, from the most mundane to the most significant. Let's consider a few scenarios.

Scenario 1: Student Performance on Standardized Tests

You are a member of a Board of Education in a small school district and have become concerned that the kids in your district are not performing well on national standardized tests. It has come to your attention that certain changes in the way subjects are taught at the elementary school level seem to bring about major improvements in these test scores. Before jumping in with both feet, you feel it necessary to collect some comparative data to support what you have heard. This calls for statistics.

Scenario 2: Fuel Consumption

You have owned the same car for five years and are concerned about your fuel consumption. Perhaps you are getting lower and lower miles per gallon. This might be an indication that it's about time to sell the old clunker and move up to one of the electronic, digital wonders of today. Surely, you must start recording your mileage and fuel consumption to examine this situation. Ah ha! This calls for statistics.

Scenario 3: Degradation of Nursing Skills

You are the duty nurse in the emergency room of a hospital and feel that nurses' skills in selected procedures degrade over time. In order to determine whether your belief is correct, you must collect enough data to warrant action on your part. This calls for statistics.

Scenario 4: Congregational Attitudes on Major Issues

You are involved in leadership role of a church denomination which has a large membership scattered throughout the country. In touring various churches in different regions of the country, you have become concerned that major issues that might cause a split in the church are developing. As a good church member, your intent is to gather enough data to support the information that you have collected on a haphazard basis during your journeys. Perhaps what you have heard is not really indicative of how congregations feel. So, a need exists for you to collect enough data to take actions, if necessary. This calls for statistics.

Scenario 5: Evaluation of Instructional Approaches

In your role as a human resources development manager within a large institution or organization, you are concerned that your methods of instruction have become outdated. You do not wish to be criticized by your management for being non-creative. Since you understand that there are many options for training, such as computer-aided, cooperative learning, and chat rooms, to name a few, you feel the need to collect enough data to be comfortable in making any recommendation for change in instructional approaches to your management. This calls for statistics.

It should be clear to you that each of the above scenarios calls for collection of some kind of data or information in order to address the specific issue. This calls for statistics.

So, what is this subject of **statistics** (*) all about anyway? Let's try a definition: Statistics is a discipline (much like mathematics or engineering are disciplines) which calls for planning and the collection, tabulation, analysis, interpretation and presentation of information. (Some might suggest that this is a definition for research. While this is true, the main emphasis here is on the data aspects of the process rather than the overall methodology, as one might encounter in research.) Now, you say, that's a mouthful, and it is. Note, however, the important first element of the discipline, namely, *planning*. Inadequate or no planning makes the results of any statistical process worthless. As is often stated, "There are liars, damn liars, and then there are statisticians." Such need not be the case. Careful planning, with detailed attention to what the issue or problem is, can provide the road map which will identify the data requirements, collection and tabulation procedures, as well as assuring a sound analysis, interpretation, and presentation of the information.

The intent of this manual is to serve the student or user of statistical procedures by building a logical structure for the discipline itself. This, hopefully, is accomplished early in this manual.

In developing examples presented in this manual, the author utilized a specific software package, namely, NCSS 97, Statistical System for Windows. An earlier version of this software (Number Cruncher Statistical Software-NCSS, 1992) was initially used because it was found to be extremely user-friendly during a three-year test period at Pepperdine University. If the reader is more familiar with other software packages, the approach utilized in this manual is still appropriate. In general, analyses using the NCSS software can be modified fairly easily for use with other statistical software, such as "Statview" and "SPSS," for both MAC and Windows platforms.

So, let's now move on to discuss some vital basic concepts in the field of statistics.

Basic Concepts

In order to drive a car you need to know something about how you start the engine, shift, use the windshield wipers and brakes, and how to turn on the emergency flasher.

In order to fly a plane, you need to know certain basics about the instrument panel and the control mechanisms.

In order to play paddle tennis, you need to know something about the rules of play, as well as how to remove the air from a regular tennis ball prior to play.

In order to use a personal computer, you need to be aware of how to turn the system on, how to start up the particular applications software package you wish to use (for example, a word processor), as well as certain basic definitions, key strokes, and possible use of a mouse.

Such is also true of understanding and using statistics. You need to be aware of certain basic concepts.

Let's start out with the most fundamental concept of all, the **analysis unit** (*). We'll refer to the analysis unit as the **AU** (*) throughout this manual. Basically, the analysis unit is that entity, thing, subject, or object, that is the basic unit of interest in addressing an issue, problem, or dilemma.

To illustrate, let's repeat the five situations presented in the previous section and see if we can identify what the AU might be.

Scenario 1: Student Performance on Standardized Tests

> You are a member of a Board of Education in a small school district and have become concerned that the kids in your district are not performing well on national standardized tests. It has come to your attention that certain changes in the way subjects are taught at the elementary school level seem to bring about major improvements in these test scores.

Test scores of students are of central importance, so the entity of interest is an elementary student, and any analysis that is conducted will examine differing impacts of instruction on the scores of the elementary school students. **An elementary student is your analysis unit**.

Scenario 2: Fuel Consumption

> You have owned the same car for five years and are concerned about your fuel consumption. Perhaps you are getting lower and lower miles per gallon. Surely, you must start recording your mileage and fuel consumption to examine this situation.

Surely, your interest here centers on data obtained from your automobile, the analysis unit for this study. **An automobile, yours, is the analysis unit.**

Scenario 3: Degradation of Nursing Skills

> You are the duty nurse in the emergency room of a hospital and feel that nurses' skills in selected procedures degrade over time. In order to determine whether your belief is correct, you must collect enough data to warrant action on your part.

Since your interest is in the degradation of nurses' skills, **a nurse is your analysis unit.**

Scenario 4: Congregational Attitudes on Major Issues

> You are involved in management of a church denomination which has a large membership scattered throughout the country. In touring various churches in different regions of the country, you have become concerned that major issues that might cause a split in the church are developing. As a good

church member, your intent is to gather enough data to support the information that you have collected on a haphazard basis during your journeys. Perhaps what you have heard is not really indicative of how congregations feel. So, a need exists for you to collect enough data to take actions, if necessary.

Since it is the feelings of the congregation members that are of interest, **your analysis unit becomes a congregation member**.

Scenario 5: Evaluation of Instructional Approaches

In your role as a human resources development manager within a large institution, you are concerned that your methods of instruction have become out dated. Since you understand that there are many options for training, such as computer-aided, cooperative learning, and chat rooms, to name a few, you feel the need to collect enough data to be comfortable in making any recommendation for change in instructional approaches to your management.

This is a tough one in which to identify an analysis unit. It might be method of instruction; but probe a bit further and ask yourself what is it you wish to assure in considering alternative methods of instruction? Certainly, if we ignore costs for the moment, it would be the impact of these alternatives on your employees, the individuals who receive the instruction. Although it's not quite as obvious as the first four examples, in this situation **the analysis unit might be an individual employee.**

Now that we have an understanding of what an analysis unit is (notice the use of the singular article "an"), let's ask ourselves a question about the *set* of analysis units of interest. But, wait, first we need to identify what we mean by the "set of analysis units of interest." We in statistics refer to this set as the **population** (*) or **universe** (*) of interest. Essentially, then, a population consists of the set of all possible analysis units of interest in studying an issue or problem. To illustrate, consider the following three situations:

You are a politician running for office and you desire information on your constituents, the registered voters.

In this scenario an analysis unit is a registered voter and the population is all registered voters in your district.

You are the superintendent of a large school district, and you are planning on implementing a new schedule for student attendance referred to as year-round-education. You have some concern over how parents of students in your district will react.

Since your concern is about parents' reactions, an analysis unit is a parent and the population consists of all parents of school age children in your school district.

You are Chief Executive Officer of a large national health maintenance organization (H.M.O.). You are planning on introducing new methods for billing and scheduling your clients. You wish to determine how your clients might react to these changes.

In this scenario, an analysis unit would be a client of the H.M.O., and the population would be all clients of your H.M.O.

Now if populations are described as above, what is a sample? Well, in its simplest terms a **sample** (*) is a sub-set of a population or less than all of the analysis units in a population. Sometimes, when your population is small, you might find it most effective to use as your sample the entire population. Notice that the definition of a sample does not imply anything about "goodness" or "representativeness." We'll say more about this issue in the chapter on sampling. Also, we will never speak of a "sample population" (an oxymoron which the author dislikes.).

So, in summary, a population is all of the AUs of interest, and a sample is some of the AUs of interest.

Now what is all this leading to? Well, in each of the scenarios presented thus far there is a critical element that we haven't discussed yet. Not all analysis units will react the same way or will yield the same data even when a well-planned approach to addressing the issue or problem has been established.[1]

What is it that makes these analysis units different and thus perhaps influences their responses? Let's call them **characteristics** (*). Characteristics of analysis units serve to differentiate among individual analysis units. Suppose we consider one of the scenarios presented earlier, namely Scenario 1:

> You are a member of a Board of Education in a small school district and have become concerned that the kids in your district are not performing well on national standardized tests. It has come to your attention that certain changes in the way subjects are taught at the elementary school level seem to bring about major improvements in these test scores.

We've already noted that the analysis unit for this situation is an elementary school child. The population is all elementary school children in this district. Now, what might be some of the characteristics that serve to differentiate among these children? Certainly gender would be one such characteristic. Three more characteristics might be ethnicity, age, and a standardized national test score. So, here we have four such characteristics that serve to differentiate among the analysis units.

Note first that the characteristics of gender and ethnicity are naturally described by words, while the characteristics of age and test score are naturally described by numerical values. In this manual, we shall refer to the first set as **attributes** (*), characteristics which are naturally described using words. The second pair we shall refer to as **variables** (*), characteristics which are naturally described (or perhaps measured) by using numerical values.

In some cases, attributes may also be analyzed as variables when the word descriptions are converted to numbers. The most common situation in which this occurs is in the analysis of survey results where the respondent is asked to express an opinion, selecting from among the options of "strongly favor," "moderately favor," "neither favor nor oppose," moderately oppose," or "strongly oppose." While characteristics in this form (often referred to as a Likert scale) are clearly attributes, it is not uncommon to convert these verbal descriptors to the numerical values of 1, 2, 3, 4, and 5, respectively, for purposes of analysis. Now we are dealing with variables. The author of this manual has some problems with assuming that the numbered Likert scores are variables. More on this topic later when we deal with inferential statistics in Chapter 7.

Now, let's move into a discussion of databases and their importance in preparing for statistical analysis of data.

1—Although research design is not a topic of this manual, the reader should be aware of the critical nature of the research design associated with any efforts to resolve issues or problems. Research methodology is a critical subject, which uses as one of its tools the statistical methods being described in this manual. Several references appear in the References/Bibliography section of this manual.

2. DATABASES

This chapter discusses what databases are, why databases are important, and issues associated with the creation of a database. The reader should note that one might consider spreadsheets (such as Excel) analogous to databases as discussed in this chapter. Fear not, the approach remains non-technical throughout.

What Is a Database?

So, what's this thing called a database? And why is it important for me to know what a database is? Simple! Data are the recorded characteristics that we use to employ statistical methods in addressing any issue or problem. A database is a file which includes all of the characteristics of interest (both attributes and variables) of a group of analysis units, as well as narrative descriptions of what the database is all about (perhaps including a name for the database). Recall the following scenario presented in Chapter 1:

> You are a member of a Board of Education in a small school district and have become concerned that the kids in your district are not performing well on national standardized tests.

We've already noted that the analysis unit for this situation is an elementary student in your school district. The population is all school children in this district. We have also noted that some of the characteristics that serve to differentiate among these kids might be gender, ethnicity, age, and the all-important standardized national test score. A database would be the file, whether on paper or in a computer, which includes each of the characteristics for each of the students. A **record** (*) would be the list of the characteristics for each of your elementary students (the AUs in this project). In addition to some specific identifier (say a coded number) for each of the students, a single record would include gender, ethnicity, age, and the standardized test score. You can probably think of other characteristics that might be included in the database, such as grade level or grade point average.

In the past, most of our databases have been typed listings of the characteristics, as well as statements about the database and each of the characteristics of interest. Any analyses associated with the database were usually conducted with desk calculators or small hand calculators.

Today, we are fortunate to have available the power of the **personal computer** (*), hereinafter referred to as the **PC** (*), to assist us in massaging data to address issues and problems of importance.

Why Databases Are Important

So, you ask, "What's the big deal about databases and the PC? Isn't it a simple thing to create a database on a PC and to perform the necessary statistical analyses?" Possibly for some individuals but probably not for others. So, in order to use this powerful PC tool it is essential that each of us understands how a database is created and how we can manage and use a database. For example, how do we add data that were missing when we originally created the database? How do we allow for missing data in some of the records? What about calculations from data in the database? What are the steps we must follow? Answers to these questions are presented in the sections and the chapters that follow.

The most important point at this stage is that the student or user understand his or her issue or problem clearly enough so that appropriate and adequate data are collected and placed in the database prior to initial analysis. Now, let's see how we go about creating a database.

Creating the Database

Before setting out to actually create a database on your PC, certain information should be available relative to this database. Some essential items are:

1. A clear description of your analysis unit, say, an elementary student.

2. An indication of numbers of digits in each of your variables. To illustrate, grade-point average usually has three digits, say 3.25; weight is usually expressed in pounds, also with three digits, say 165; and, test scores are generally expressed in three or less digits, say 95.

3. Precise names for all of your attributes. It is clear that SEX or GENDER will be male or female, but what about marital status or ethnicity? In order to set up your database, specific word descriptions for each attribute are essential.

4. Any narrative description of your sample or population of analysis units. For example, the sample is a group of elementary school students in District A.

Although many statistical software packages are available, for purposes of this manual, we have been using the NCSS 97, Statistical System for Windows (Hintze, 1997). Users of this manual could certainly employ other statistical software with which they are familiar, such as Statview and SPSS (please see references). Dependence on the NCSS system will be minimized during the balance of this manual.

Now, let's consider some additional terminology with which we must be familiar as we embark on the journey of database creation.

Creating databases for specific statistical software packages is usually a function of the specific software, although many of the newer statistical software packages permit an individual to create a database in one application software (such as EXCEL, Lotus 123, Paradox, or Access) and then import the database into the format necessary to conduct statistical analyses. It is not the intent of this manual to delve further into the creation of such databases. However, creation of the database in such software makes it possible to utilize whatever statistical software is available. The reader is referred to statistical packages for such a process.

Once your database has been created, you should print out a copy of the data so that you can check the accuracy of the data typed in. Remember, GARBAGE IN, GARBAGE OUT. This is especially true when dealing with statistical analyses. To illustrate, in inputting test scores, ranging from, say, 0–100, a heavy hand might inadvertently input an 850 instead of an 85. Such an error would create havoc in analyzing the data, for example, by resulting in a statistical measure which is wrong. The author of this manual strongly recommends that the person performing analyses use as many visual representations as possible. Many times, a data entry error will be evident from a chart or graph. Chapter 4 discusses selected graphic displays.

Appendices E and F provide examples of listings of the characteristics' input for two specific databases, namely 2SCH4 and ENGSCO, both of which will be used throughout this Manual.

3. SAMPLING

In the previous chapter the reader was exposed to the concept of "database" and its importance in statistical analysis. We now consider issues associated with how the analysis units are selected.

You may well ask, "What's the big deal about sampling? Can't we just select a sample and then say what we want to about the population?" NO! NO! NO! Understanding the sampling process is essential if one is to make an attempt to say something about the population based upon information from the sample. This concept of generalizing from a sample to the population from which the sample was selected is referred to as **statistical inference** (*) and is the subject considered in Chapter 7 of this Manual.

It is essential to understand how the sample is selected and how the population of analysis units is organized (either naturally or artificially). These are both important concepts if one is to go beyond describing the sample (Chapter 6) to generalizing to the population from which the sample was selected (Chapter 7).

The sections that follow address the two concepts of sample selection and population organization.

Selecting the Sample

Although one might consider numerous approaches to sample selection, only three are discussed in this section: random, systematic, and purposive.

Random Sampling

The basis for making statements about populations based upon samples assumes, in almost all cases, that the sample has been randomly drawn from the population of interest. So how do we draw a **random** (*) sample?

First, it is necessary for the analysis units in the population of interest to be available for selection in the sample (this is not always the case and should be considered during the planning process for the project). You might say, "What an idiotic statement to make. Obviously all analysis units must be available for selection!" It is certainly obvious but not always true.

Essentially, there must exist a **sampling frame** (*) of the analysis units. A sampling frame, in its simplest form, is a listing that identifies all analysis units of interest in your project or study. One might say that the sampling frame lists every AU in the population of interest. The sampling frame may or may not include specific characteristics of an AU. For example, a telephone directory constitutes a possible sampling frame. While listing the name, address (usually), and phone number, no other characteristics of the AUs appear in this sampling frame. The sampling frame might be in a file cabinet or in a computerized database. Regardless of where and in what form it exists, the entire population must be accessible for sample selection.

Second, an identification number (ID number) must be either assigned or capable of being assigned to each analysis unit in the population. With these two criteria met, it is now possible to select a random sample.

The process is conceptually quite simple. Assume that you put each person's (ID) number on a ping-pong ball and then put all the ping-pong balls in a large bowl. The bowl is then agitated for some time and a single ball is selected from the bowl, possibly by dropping through an opening at the bottom of the bowl, much like what one sees in a bingo game. The analysis unit corresponding to the identification (ID) number on this ball is the first AU in your sample. This approach is analogous to a lottery. The process is repeated until the number of AUs needed for your sample has been reached. Note that in this process, particularly if the population is small, each AU has a changing likelihood (probability) of being in the sample. To illustrate, if there are only 10 AUs in the population, the likelihood that, by this process, a particular one of the ten will be selected first is 1 in 10 or 10%. Now, once the first AU (ping pong ball) has been selected, only 9 remain to be selected, so the likelihood of any one of the 9 being selected is 1 in 9 or 11.1%. This process which we have just described is referred to as **random sampling without replacement** (*). Such a process assures that no AU can be selected in the sample more than once.

It should also be clear that, if the population is quite large, say 5,000, and this process of sampling without replacement is followed, the likelihood of selecting any of the AUs first is 1 in 5,000 or .02%. Once the first AU has been selected, 4,999 remain. The likelihood of selecting any one of the remaining 4,999 is 1 in 4,999, or also .02%.

In reality, this lottery-type approach is not used often, if ever, in selecting a random sample. Two options that are most frequently used are selecting the AU through use of a table of random numbers or allowing a computer, through software program such as NCSS, SPSS, SAS, and Statview, to select the random numbers and then identify the AUs within the sampling frame.

Let's consider first how one might develop a table of random numbers. Assume that you have ten ping-pong balls with the numbers 0 through 9 marked on the balls, with each number occurring only once. Following the same procedure described above, the bowl containing the ping pong balls can be agitated and a single ping pong ball ejected from the bowl. This number is then recorded and the ball placed back in the bowl. The process is repeated, with the number on the ball being recorded each time and the ball being replaced in the bowl each time. Let's assume that the sequence of the first ten numbers which have been recorded is 3460 3547 20. If one were looking for a four digit random number, one might select 3460 or 4603 or 6035 or 0354, depending upon the rule selected prior to initiating the sampling process. This rule would then be followed throughout the balance of the sample selection.

Now, this process leads us to a good definition for **random sampling** (*). It seems to be a process in which each analysis unit, at each selection of an analysis unit, has an equal likelihood (probability) of being in the sample, where this probability changes if sampling is without replacement.

Systematic Sampling

Frequently, for practical or administrative reasons, the selection of a random sample is quite difficult. Under these circumstances and, if the AUs are arranged in some order (such as in a telephone directory or a membership list), it makes more sense to use a systematic approach in sample selection.

Basically, **systematic sampling** (*) is a procedure whereby the individual AUs are taken at fixed intervals, say every 20th AU, from a listing of the population (the sampling frame).

To illustrate, suppose a sample of teachers is desired from a large school district and random selection would be an administrative nightmare. If a 5% sample (for whatever reason) is desired, then a systematic sample would involve taking every 20th teacher from the list. The requirement is that the first teacher in the sample be randomly selected from among the first 20 teachers in the list. This process is referred to as **systematic sampling with a random start** (*) . One might also select a random starting point anywhere in a list and then continue with the selection of every, say 20th, AU until returning to the starting point in the list.

Suppose, now, that the random number selected is a 7. The first teacher in the sample would be teacher number 7. Then, because of the systematic nature of the sampling, the balance of the sample would consist of teachers 27, 47, 67, 87, and so on until the total sample had been selected.

This process might be followed, for example, if one were to desire a sample of phone numbers from a telephone directory. Clearly random sampling would also be quite tedious and time consuming. Hence, the use of systematic sampling with a random start.

Suppose the population consisted of 1,000 AUs. If a 5% sample were desired, then a sample would consist of 50 AUs (1,000x05 = 50). Since the population consists of 1,000 AUs, using a systematic sample would yield 20 possible different samples of 50 AUs each (1,000÷50 = 20). The starting point for selection of a sample would be a randomly drawn number between 1 and 20. If one were to select the 50 AUs randomly, more than 100,000 such different samples could be selected. Quite a difference.

A word of warning: if any of the characteristics of interest in the study are related in any way whatsoever to the position of the AU in the sampling frame, then systematic sampling should be used with caution. For example, suppose that a firm allocates a final digit of 0 to any account receivable whose value is $10,000 or more. All other accounts are included in the listing in the order incurred. Any systematic sampling procedure that would deliberately include or not include an AU with a last digit of 0 should be viewed with caution. This is a situation in which stratified sampling (to be discussed later in this chapter) might be an appropriate approach.

Purposive Sampling

Purposive sampling is a process in which certain AUs are included in the sample "on purpose." Generalization to the population of interest is, therefore, always questionable.

Population Organization

Frequently, the population of analysis units may be either naturally organized into what we shall call **clusters** (*) or may be artificially organized into what we shall call **strata** (*). Under these two situations, the selection of a random sample from the total population may not be possible or desirable. The balance of this section discusses these two population groupings.

Clusters

Clusters may be defined as natural groupings of the analysis units. Perhaps the simplest illustration can be given when we consider the analysis unit as a student in a school district. A natural grouping of students within a school district might be by school building, the cluster. If the analysis unit were a teacher, school buildings would again be considered as clusters of teachers.

Since there is no sampling frame or list of all school teachers in the United States, one might find it most efficient to sample school districts (clusters) prior to selecting a sample of teachers. Generally speaking, school districts maintain lists of the teachers employed within the district.

Another example might be to consider a national health care organization, say a health maintenance organization with facilities located in virtually every state. If the analysis unit in this situation were a nurse, individual facilities could be considered as clusters of nurses. Or, if the analysis unit were a patient, individual facilities could again be considered as a cluster of patients.

Consider a large national health club. If the analysis unit is a member of the club, then an individual club, such as the Spectrum Club, might be considered as a cluster of members.

Another illustration might arise when considering students within a large university system as the analysis units. The individual campuses could be considered as clusters of students.

The real value of cluster sampling occurs when the analysis units are not available for sampling in a single sampling frame. While the theoretical issues associated with cluster sampling are beyond the scope of this manual, the reader can consult the references for a text on sampling theory.

Strata

Frequently when sampling, it may be desired to assure that certain types of analysis units are included in the sample. Under these conditions, it is conceivable that the analysis units could be grouped into mutually exclusive strata. Mutually exclusive strata implies that an analysis unit can be a member of one and only one stratum.

To illustrate, suppose a random sample of 1,000 teachers was to be taken from the population of public school teachers throughout the United States. First of all, no sampling frame that includes all U.S. teachers exists. If one did, however, it is conceivable that many of the large school districts might not be represented in the sample. To assure representation of some teachers within school districts of various sizes, it is possible to stratify the school districts by size, a process that is currently utilized by both the National Center for Education Statistics and the National Education Association in their national surveys of public school teachers. (See **Status of the American Public School Teacher**, National Educational Association, Washington, D.C., 1997.) It should be recognized that the strata may differ in numbers of analysis units within each stratum. Sampling can either be in proportion to the number of AUs in each stratum or disproportionate. In the latter case adjustments must be made in generalizing to the population.

Another illustration might occur when a politician, wishing to assure representation from all ethnic groups, has the sampling frame of AUs stratified by ethnicity and possibly gender of the registered voter.

At times, stratified and cluster sampling may need to be performed together in what is referred to as multi-stage sampling. The best illustration of this is the one in which the analysis unit is a public school teacher. Since no sampling frame exists of all public school teachers within the United States, a logical process would be to group school districts by size of, say, enrollment. This constitutes the first stage of the sampling, in which strata are developed. Within each strata, school districts may then be selected according to some random process. These school districts constitute clusters of the analysis units, namely, the teachers. Then, from within the school districts selected by this random process, teachers can next be selected randomly or on a systematic basis with a random start. (McCall, 1982)

This chapter has highlighted basic concepts about the sampling process. Any individual intending to select a sample should give careful consideration to how the analysis units are organized and whether or not a simple random sample can be selected. Again, it is not the intent of this manual to delve into the more complex sampling designs, only to make the individual aware of the possibilities that exist in sampling.

The next chapter presents information on tabular and graphic display of sample or population data.

4. TABULAR AND GRAPHIC DISPLAYS

This chapter provides a description of numerous ways in which graphic presentations can be utilized in reporting on study results. The reader is urged to consult available software, such as Lotus 123, Excel, Paradox or PowerPoint, to develop unusual and professional-looking charts and graphs. An excellent series of examples can be found in Tufte (1983, 1990, and 1998).

This chapter displays examples that are most frequently employed in basic descriptive statistics. The following examples are presented with a brief discussion of each:

Distributions and Cumulative Distributions

>   Line Diagrams
>
>   Bar Charts
>
>   Stacked Bar Charts
>
>   Pie Diagrams
>
>   Scatter Plots
>
>   Pareto Diagrams

Distributions and Cumulative Distributions

A frequency distribution identifies the frequency (number of cases or counts) or percentage (relative frequency) with which specific categories of an attribute or intervals of a variable occur. An example of a frequency distribution appears as Exhibit 4.1, where the analysis unit is a school counselor in a given school district and the variable is the number of years employed as a school psychologist.

EXHIBIT 4.1 YEARS EMPLOYED AS A SCHOOL COUNSELOR

Years (1)	Number of Persons (2)	Percentage (3)	Cumulative Number* (4)	Cumulative Percentage* (5)
0 – 3	31	18.1%	31	18.1%
4 – 7	31	18.1	62	36.3
8 – 11	36	21.1	98	57.3
12 – 15	25	14.6	123	71.9
16 – 19	25	14.6	148	86.5
20 – 23	10	5.8	158	92.4
24 – 27	7	4.1	165	96.5
28 – 31	3	1.8	168	98.2
32 – 35	2	1.2	170	99.4
36 – 39	1	0.6	171	100.0

* Cumulative number and cumulative percentage of persons less than or equal to the upper number of years in each class interval.

Exhibit 4.2 identifies monthly rental income and associated expenses for a rental unit in a winter resort area.

EXHIBIT 4.2 RENTAL INCOME AND EXPENSES, JANUARY–MAY 1996

MONTH	RENTAL INCOME	EXPENSES
January	$1,809	$670
February	1,539	570
March	710	263
April	570	211
May	130	48

These two exhibits contain data that illustrate the various types of graphic displays that follow, with the exception of the scatter plots and the Pareto Diagram.

Line Diagrams

Exhibits 4.3 is a plot of the number of counselors versus years of employment. Exhibit 4.4 is a plot of the percentage of counselors versus years of employment. These two plots are essentially the same, except the second plot converts the numbers to percentages. These plots are based upon columns (2) and (3) in Exhibit 4.1 plotted against column (1).

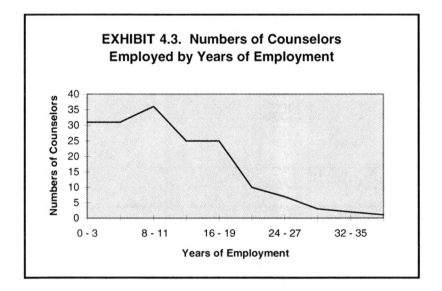

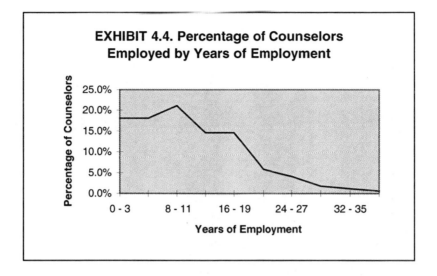

Exhibit 4.5 is a plot of the cumulative number of counselors, classified by years of employment. Exhibit 4.6 is a plot of the cumulative percentage of counselors, classified by years of employment. These plots are based upon data from Exhibit, 4.1, namely, columns (4) and (5) as compared with column (1).

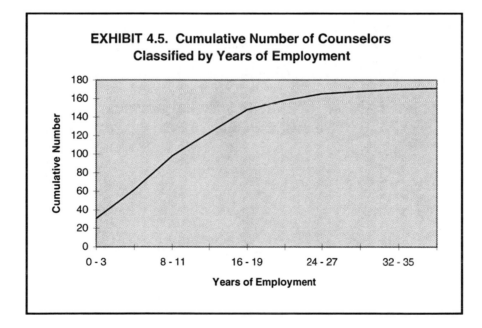

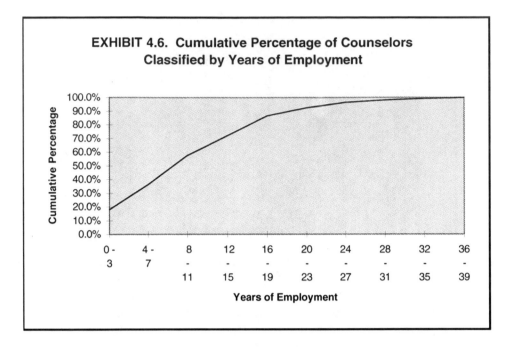

EXHIBIT 4.6. Cumulative Percentage of Counselors Classified by Years of Employment

Exhibit 4.7 is a line diagram in which two sets of data, rental income and expenses, are plotted on the same graph against the specific month in which the income and expenses were incurred. The base scale is taken from Exhibit 4.2, column (1), the rental income from column (2) and the expenses from column (3).

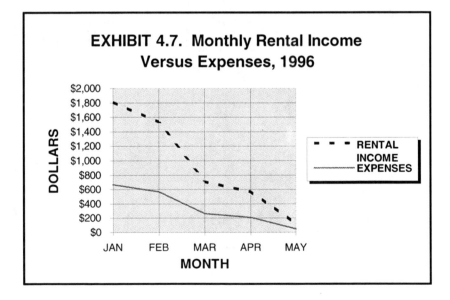

EXHIBIT 4.7. Monthly Rental Income Versus Expenses, 1996

Bar Charts

Exhibit 4.8 is referred to as a 3-D (three dimensional) bar chart and reflects the data from column (2) versus column (1) in Exhibit 4.1. Bar charts can also be two-dimensional.

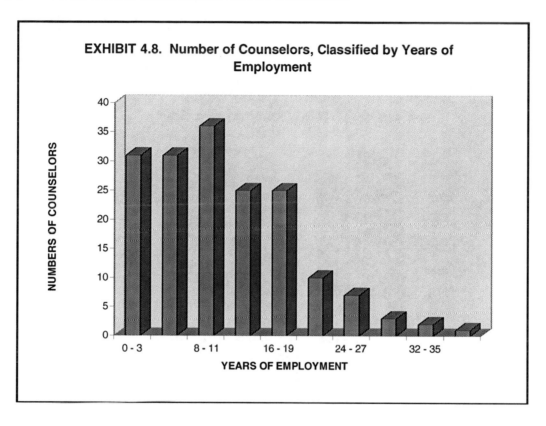

Exhibit 4.9 allows for a visual comparison of the rental income and expenses for each of the five months presented in Exhibit 2. This is also a three dimensional bar chart. Bar charts may also be presented horizontally ("landscape view" in computer parlance) instead of vertically, although the vertical mode ("portrait view") is more common.

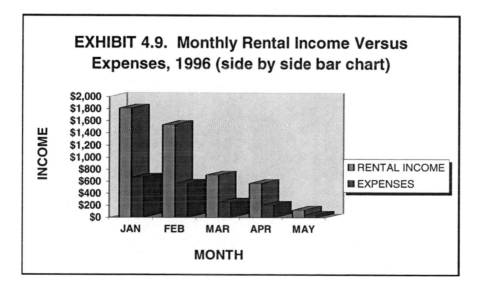

Stacked Bar charts

There are times when side-by-side bar charts take up too much space or when they don't clearly carry the message of the data. Under those conditions a stacked bar chart is sometimes used, as in Exhibit 4.10. In this bar chart the rental income series appears as the lower part of the bar, with the expenses data being "stacked" on top of the rental income.

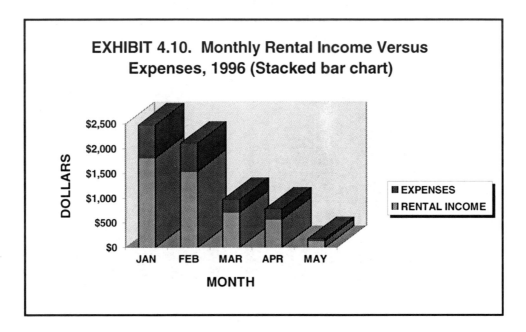

EXHIBIT 4.10. Monthly Rental Income Versus Expenses, 1996 (Stacked bar chart)

Pie Diagrams

There may be times when it is of interest to consider a given set of data in terms of percentages. In Exhibit 4.11, from the data in Exhibit 4.2, for the month of January, the net income (rental income less expenses) and expenses can be plotted as a pie diagram and then each expressed as a percentage of this total.

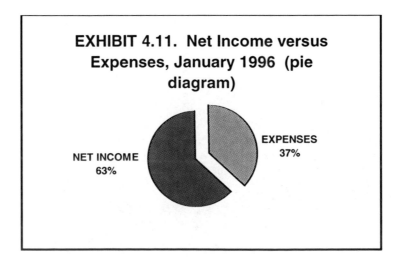

EXHIBIT 4.11. Net Income versus Expenses, January 1996 (pie diagram)

Scatter Plots

Scatter plots are used to give a visual representation of the possible relationship between two variables. Examples of scatter plots are given in Exhibits 6.3–6.9 in Chapter 6.

Pareto Diagrams

A Pareto diagram is nothing more than a bar chart with the items being arranged in either ascending or descending order, based upon the vertical scale values. Exhibit 4.12 is based upon information taken from a survey in which the respondents were asked to rate items as **Very Important, Important, Neither Important nor Unimportant, Unimportant**, and **Very Unimportant**. The information in Exhibit 4.12 rank orders the top five items by the percentage of respondents selected **Very Important**. For example, Item 5 was rated **Very Important** by approximately 75% of the respondents, and so on. This process enables the person analyzing these survey results to have a visual impression of how items are ordered. One could develop a Pareto diagram for all of the items on the instrument and note where there is a definite drop in the observed percentages.

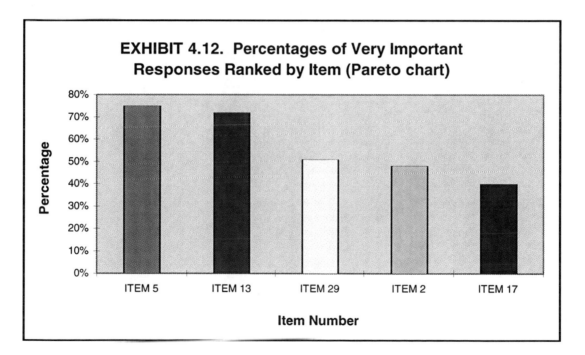

EXHIBIT 4.12. Percentages of Very Important Responses Ranked by Item (Pareto chart)

5. DISTRIBUTIONS

As a lead into a discussion of distributions, let's consider some basic elements of probability. Then, we'll look at two important distributions, namely, the binomial and multinomial. This chapter concludes with a section on cross-tabulations.

Basic Probability

Everything we do in life has associated with it a probability that the event will occur. How often have we encountered statements like "There is a 90% chance that it will rain today" or, "There is a 70% chance that it will snow at Mammoth Mountain this weekend"? When we leave home, there is a probability that we may be involved in an automobile accident or that we might run into someone we haven't seen for years. Of course, we probably (?) don't know what these probabilities are, but they do exist. When we take out life insurance, the premiums are usually dependent upon our sex and age. These premiums are determined by how long people of our same age and sex have lived in the past. In other words, there is a probability that you will live to be a certain age, with that probability decreasing as you get older. (A reviewer of this manual pointed out that after a certain age, the probability actually increases.)

All of these examples illustrate that probabilities exist, whether they be known or unknown to you. Appendix B is a brief discussion of elementary probability theory for those who are interested in pursuing the basic concepts in more detail. A review of this appendix is not, however, essential for your understanding of the materials that follow.

Distributions and Cumulative Distributions

Another important concept in statistics is that of **distributions** (*). We speak of the distribution of an attribute or the distribution of a variable. To illustrate, for the attribute SEX, the following table tells us how this characteristic is distributed in a sample of 200 respondents to a survey:

SEX	Frequency	Percentage
Female	125	62.5%
Male	75	37.5%
Total	**200**	**100.0%**

This table gives the frequency distribution and the percentage distribution for the attribute SEX. The 200 cases are distributed with 125 females and 75 males. Another way to state this would be that the attribute SEX is distributed with 62.5% being female and 37.5% being male.

Now, let's consider examining distributions for a variable, say AGE, of the respondents to a different survey. The table which follows indicates the number (frequency) and percentage of respondents in each age category, group, or **interval** (*).

AGE CATEGORIES (1)	Frequency(2)	Percentage (3)
20-29	75	25.0%
30-39	85	28.3%
40-49	125	41.7%
50 or more	15	5.0%
Totals	300	100.0%

The above table tells us that age is distributed across four categories or intervals, ranging from 75 respondents in the age group, 20–29, to only 15 respondents in the age group, 50 more. One might also restate this is terms of percentages: 25.0% of the respondents were in the age group, 20–29, while in the age group, 50 or more, there were only 5.0% of the respondents. In the first statement, we are discussing frequencies and in the second, percentages. If we consider column (1) and column (2) in the above table together, the pair of columns is referred to as the **frequency distribution** (*). If we consider column (1) and column (3) together, the pair of columns is referred to as the **percentage distribution** (*).

When we are dealing with a description of the distribution of variables, one might be interested in describing the number, or percentage, less than a given group or value. For example, consider the distribution of AGE again as now given in the table that follows.

Age Categories	Frequency	Percentage	Cumulative Frequency	Cumulative Percentage
20 - 29	75	25.0%	75	25.0%
30 - 39	85	28.3%	160	53.3%
40 - 49	125	41.7%	285	95.0%
50 or more	15	5.0%	300	100.0%
TOTAL	300	100%	300	100%

When combined with the first column, the last two columns are referred to, respectively, as the **cumulative frequency distribution** (*) and **cumulative percentage distribution** (*). This means that each column gives you the cumulative frequency or percentage of respondents with ages less than the given age category or interval. For example, the 285 in the 4th column and the row representing ages 40–49 indicates that 285 of the respondents were below the "50 or more" category. In the last column for the 30–39 age category, the 53.3% figure indicates that 53.3% of the respondents were of ages less than the 40–49 category.

Binomial Distribution

Now, let's consider the simplest of all distributions, the **binomial** (*). Binomial means **two names**. This distribution applies when dealing with an attribute in which the attribute is **dichotomous** (*), meaning there are only two alternatives or classifications, such as SEX: male or female. Another example of a binomial distribution might be the result when a coin is tossed, yielding heads or tails. Yet another might occur when, on a survey, the respondent is asked to indicate an opinion on an attitudinal issue by checking a YES or a NO. In each of these cases, the resulting distribution of the attribute could be expressed as either frequencies or percentages. One might, for example, see a table such as the following in which the YES or NO responses for the 300 respondents are summarized.

RESPONSE	Number	Percentage
YES	75	25.0%
NO	225	75.0%
TOTAL	300	100.0%

In this situation, 75 out of 300 (25.0%) responded with a YES and 225 out of 300 (75.0%) with a NO.

Multinomial

If we now allow for the fact that attributes may possess more than two alternatives, say when we consider the distribution of ethnic groups within a metropolitan area, then we must define a new type of distribution. This we shall refer to as a **multinomial distribution** (*), meaning **many names**. Any attribute that assigns the AUs among more than two categories can be considered as a multinomial. Suppose, for example, we classify our AUs in terms of academic levels. The distribution of academic levels might look like Exhibit 5.1.

EXHIBIT 5.1. Distribution of Academic Levels		
Highest Academic Level Achieved	Number	Percentage
High School	55	27.5%
Bachelor's	95	47.5%
Master's	35	17.5%
Doctorate	15	7.5%
TOTALS	200	100%

From this exhibit it can be seen that 95 of the 200 AUs possess bachelor's degrees. This represents 47.5% (95/200) of this group of AUs.

Consider for this same group of 200 their responses to an opinion item on a survey where there are five possible responses. Exhibit 5.2 summarizes the distribution of responses.

EXHIBIT 5.2. Distribution of Opinions on an Attitudinal Item		
ATTITUDE	**Number**	**Percentage**
Strongly Favor	45	22.5%
Favor	95	47.5%
Neither Favor nor Oppose	15	7.5%
Oppose	20	10.0%
Strongly Oppose	25	12.5%
TOTALS	200	100.0%

The distribution of responses, or attitudes, given in Exhibit 5.2 is considered a multinomial distribution. It can be seen that 15 of the 200 respondents "Neither Favored nor Opposed" the given item. This represents 7.5% (15/200) of the respondents.

Two-Way Distributions (Cross-Tabs)

If one were to reexamine the data in Exhibit 5.2, we might refer to this as a **one-way table** (*) inasmuch as the characteristic of interest is being examined in only one way, namely, over all responses to a single attitudinal item on the survey. Suppose, for the sake of discussion, the investigator wished to examine the same distribution of responses as in Exhibit 5.2 when considering the SEX of the individuals. Such a tabular set of results might look like the data in Exhibit 5.3.

EXHIBIT 5.3. Distribution of Opinions on an Attitudinal Item when Considering Sex			
ATTITUDE	**Male**	**Female**	**Total**
Strongly Favor	20	25	**45**
Favor	45	50	**95**
Neither Favor nor Oppose	10	5	15
Oppose	15	5	20
Strongly Oppose	20	5	25
TOTALS	**110**	**90**	**200**

The frequencies that are in the last column, such as 45 and 95, and the last row, such as 110 and 90, are referred to as **marginal frequencies** (*). The frequencies within the body of the exhibit, such as 20, 25, and 45, are referred to as **cell frequencies** (*). **Cells** (*) in tables, such as Exhibit 5.3, may include not only frequencies but also percentages. The number 45, which is boxed in Exhibit 5.3, tells us that 45 of the responses were from males who favored the item. Exhibit 5.3 presents the frequencies with which males and females responded to the five attitudinal categories. For example, of the 100 males, 15 indicated that they "Oppose" the item while 20 indicate they "Strongly Favor" the item. On the other hand, of the 90 females, 5 "Oppose" the item while 25 indicate they "Strongly Favor" the item. It should be clear that other statements could be made using the marginal and cell frequencies.

Now let's suppose that one might be interested in discussing percentages rather than frequencies. It should be evident that we could discuss the percentage of responses in the total sample without consideration of the SEX of the individuals, as in Exhibit 5.2. We could also specify that 55% of the sample (110/200) were male and 45% of the sample (90/200) were females. There are, in fact, a number of different ways to express the frequencies in exhibits such as 5.3. Exhibit 5.4 presents a total of four entries for each SEX and ATTITUDE combination.

EXHIBIT 5.4. Distribution of Opinions on an Attitudinal Item when Considering Sex (Frequencies and Percentages)			
ATTITUDE	**Male**	**Female**	**TOTALS**
Strongly Favor	20 44% 18% 10%	25 56% 28% 12%	45　23%
Favor	45 47% 41% 23%	50 53% 56% 25%	95　48%
Neither Favor nor Oppose	10 67% 9% 5%	5 33% 6% 3%	15　8%
Oppose	15 75% 14% 8%	5 25% 6% 3%	20　10%
Strongly Oppose	20 80% 18% 10%	5 20% 6% 3%	25　12%
TOTALS	**110 (55%)**	**90 (45%)**	**200**

Let's first of all indicate what the entries in each cell of Exhibit 5.4 represent. Recall that a cell is the position in Exhibit 5.4 in which a row entry, say FAVOR, intersects with a column entry, say, MALE. Exhibit 5.4 has 10 cells, since there are two columns labeled SEX and five rows labeled ATTITUDE (2x5 = 10). For the cell indicating the MALES who responded with a "Favor" opinion, there are four entries. This cell in Exhibit 5.4 is indicated by a box. Each of the four boxed-in cell entries is repeated below and its meaning identified:

45　　there were 45 MALES who responded in "Favor" of the item

47%　　47% (45/95) of those in "Favor" of the item were MALES (45); note that the percentages across each row add to 100% (except for possible rounding considerations).

41%   of the 110 MALES who responded, 41% (45/110) were in "Favor" of the item; note that the percentages for this third entry add down the column to 100% (except for possible rounding considerations).

23%   of the 200 respondents, 23% (45/200) were MALES who were in "Favor" of the item; note that if you add the fourth entry in each of the 10 cells in the exhibit, the result will be 100% (except for possible rounding considerations).

The percentages in the last column of Exhibit 5.4 represent, as in Exhibit 5.2, the percentage of all respondents (regardless of SEX) who selected each of the five attitudinal categories. These percentages add to 100% (except for possible rounding considerations). The two percentages in the last row of Exhibit 5.4 represent the percentage of all respondents who were MALE or FEMALE, independent of attitude.

Distributions of this type are referred to as **two-way distributions** (*), **contingency tables** (*), **cross-tabulations** (*), or simply **cross-tabs** (*).

Now, let's consider one of the databases that appears in the appendices to this manual, namely, 2SCH4. (NOTE: as stated earlier, the printouts in Appendix E, 2SCH4, are associated with analyses using the NCSS software package. This database will be referred to numerous times throughout the balance of this manual. It is advisable to read the brief description of the database given on page E.1.)

For this database, a cross-tabulation appears on page E.19. This cross-tabulation, in a slightly modified form, is reproduced as Exhibit 5.5 below. Much of the structure of the cross-tabulation on page E.19 is related to the format of the NCSS statistical software output. Other statistical software will have slightly different output and formatting. However, the process for interpreting the entries within the cross-tabs would apply to any software output for this type of descriptive statistics. Entries for each cell are clearly marked. This database consists of 224 students from a single high school. The data have been collected for three graduating classes over a three-year period. The columns in Exhibit 5.5, describing the attribute SEX, are clearly labeled MALE and FEMALE. The three rows associated with the year of graduation are labeled 1982, 1983, and 1984. Since there are two columns and three rows of data, there are six cells of data in Exhibit 5.5.

EXHIBIT 5.5. Distributions of Students, Males and Females, Graduating from a Given High School over Three Years

YEAR	Male	Female	TOTAL
1982	34	31	65
	52.3%	47.7%	100.0%
	29.1%	29.0%	29.0%
	15.2%	13.8%	29.0%
1983	39	**43**	82
	47.6%	**52.4%**	100.0%
	33.3%	**40.2%**	36.6%
	17.4%	**19.2%**	36.6%
1984	44	33	77
	57.1%	42.9%	100.0%
	37.6%	30.8%	34.4%
	19.6%	14.7%	34.4%
TOTAL	**117**	**107**	**224**
	52.2%	**47.8%**	**100.0%**
	100.0%	**100.0%**	**100.0%**
	52.2%	**47.8%**	**100.0%**

Now, let's consider how we might interpret four entries in the cell representing FEMALES graduating in 1983. The following description gives meaning to each of these four numbers:

43   There were 43 FEMALES in this study who graduated during 1983.

52.4%   This is a row percentage and indicates that, of those graduating in 1983, 52.4% (43/82) were FEMALES.

40.2%   This is a column percentage and indicates that, of the 107 females in the study, 40.2% (43/107) graduated in 1983.

19.2%   This is a table (or cell) percentage and indicates that, of the 224 students in the study, 19.2% (43/224) were females graduating in 1983.

From the above examples, it should be clear that we are able to discuss distributions of various characteristics alone or, as in the latter two examples, in a cross tabulation. More on cross-tabs in Chapter 7 when we look at chi-square (χ^2). One of the more well known distributions not discussed in this chapter is referred to as the **normal distribution** (*), and is discussed in detail in Chapter 7.

6. DESCRIPTIVE STATISTICS

The researcher in the field of education may be interested in describing the characteristics of the analysis units (AUs) of interest, such as a teacher, a pupil, a school, a school district, a voter, or an institution, such as a hospital or a church congregation. It is not enough to collect your data and then present your findings with charts or tables. The researcher must be able to discuss these data, whether they are related to a sample or a population. Typical questions that might be asked are:

1. Are values of the variables of interest close together or are they widely scattered?

2. Is it possible to describe whether the data are concentrated more at one value than another?

3. What is the shape of the frequency distribution? Is it symmetrical? Are the AUs evenly distributed across values of the variable or categories of an attribute?

4. Does there appear to be any relationship among the characteristics?

Descriptive measures are **statistics** (*) or **parameters** (*) that the researcher can use to respond to such questions and to describe research findings. Statistics are descriptive measures associated with samples, and parameters are the corresponding descriptive measures associated with a population. These descriptive measures, be they for a sample or a population, provide a basis for summarizing information contained in the attributes and variables associated with the AUs of interest. In general, these descriptive measures fall into four categories:

1. Central tendency: How are the characteristics concentrated?

2. Variability, variation, or dispersion: How are the characteristics scattered or dispersed?

3. Positional or relative: For a given characteristic, what are the relative positions or locations of individual AUs within a set of data?

4. Relational or association: Are any two or more of the characteristics related to each other?

More specifically, **measures of central tendency** (*) identify where the values of the characteristics of interest tend to be concentrated. These include the **arithmetic mean** (*) (**average** (*)), **median** (*), and **mode** (*). Certainly we have all used the arithmetic mean many times, for example, to describe an average grade we have received in a course.

Measures of variation or dispersion (*) identify how the characteristics of interest are scattered within the sample or population. These include the **range** (*), **interquartile range** (*), **average deviation** (*), and **standard deviation** (*). We will see that these measures are an indication of the homogeneity or heterogeneity of a set of data. We understand what it means when a teacher says that the grades on a specific test ranged from 65 to 100. A similar group of students might have grades on the same test that ranged from 90 to 100. We refer to the first group as being more heterogeneous than the second. Conversely, we refer to the second group as being more homogeneous than the first.

Positional or relative measures (*) indicate the relative position of a particular observation or group of observations within a sample or population. Among these measures to be discussed are **percentiles** (*) and

standard scores (*). Frequently, when an individual takes a standardized test, the raw score is given as well as the corresponding percentile, which indicates what percentage of those taking the test received lower scores.

Relational or association measures (*) indicate the extent to which two or more characteristics are or are not related. Among such measures discussed will be **correlation** (*) and **regression** (*). We would certainly expect that grades obtained in high school (e.g., the grade point average) would be somehow related to grades obtained in college.

ALL EXHIBITS ARE LOCATED AT THE END OF THIS CHAPTER.

Central Tendency

Measures of central tendency are descriptive quantities, determined from your data, which tell us something about how the characteristics of interest are concentrated. While there are many more than the three discussed below, experience has shown that these three are the most widely used in educational research.

Arithmetic Mean

Perhaps the best known measure of central tendency is the arithmetic mean , generally referred to as the mean. The arithmetic mean, or simple average, is obtained by adding up all values of the variable (note, **not** an attribute) of interest and then dividing by the number of AUs represented by that total.

Consider, for example, the distribution of "years of tenure" for six teachers in a given school district, as presented in Exhibit 6.1. It can be seen that the sum of the six (n = 6) "years of tenure" is 30. When this total is divided by 6, the resulting average is seen to be 5 years.

You will note that there is a new symbol (S) in the referenced example. This and other symbols are described in Appendix A which presents "Some Basic Arithmetic Notations."

In Appendix E there are printouts from a database referred to as 2SCH4. One can determine the average of the 224 AUs' SAT (Scholastic Aptitude Test) Verbal score from the Detail Report in the Descriptive Statistics window . The arithmetic mean is seen to be 426.5179. We really don't need all the digits to the right of the decimal point. Let's agree to use one more digit in our summary measures than the raw data. Hence, we would report the average SAT verbal score as 426.5.

It is standard practice in statistical circles to use the Greek letter mu (μ) to represent a population mean and the symbol X-bar ($\overline{X}$) to represent the sample mean. More on this distinction in Chapter 7 when inference is discussed.

Median

The median is the middle value of the variable of interest when the values for the variable have been ranked (ordered) from high to low or from low to high. For the tenure data in Exhibit 6.1 the ranked values would be

$$2 \quad 3 \quad 5 \quad 6 \quad 6 \quad 8$$

Since there is an even number of observations, it is usual to take the average of the two middle values and call this the median. For this small set of data, the median would be between 5 and 6. The median is reported as 5.5.

For the 2SCH4 database in Appendix E, the SAT Verbal median is seen to be 430 . Note that the median is also identified as the 50th percentile (more on this point in the section on positional measures).

Although there are symbols for a population and sample median, we'll just stick with the verbal description. So, we now have two measures of central tendency. Let's look at the third.

Mode

At times one value, or group of values, of a variable or an attribute occurs more often than any other value or group of values. We refer to this measure as the mode (most often). A mode, or modal value, may not exist in a data set.

For our "years of tenure" example in Exhibit 6.1, although weak, the mode is 6. For the SAT Verbal score in Appendix E, we cannot identify a single modal value but can conclude that the modal class (with 55 observations) is 417.1429 to 482.8572. Who's kidding whom on the use of decimals. We'd be better off to state that the modal class is from 418 to 482, since 418 is the lowest possible SAT in the class (sometimes referred to as **interval** (*)) and 482 is the largest possible SAT in the class. Use the mode with care in describing your data; i.e., when there is an indication that one value or one group stands out as having a larger number of observations.

Observations

To obtain an average, one must be dealing with variables. It should be clear that no average value can be calculated for an attribute (it would be strange to describe the average ethnic value as 2.45, although it has been done). As a matter of fact, a good test of whether you have a variable or an attribute is whether a meaningful mean can be calculated. Use of the three measures together, coupled with some of the pictorial materials in Chapter 4, should provide the researcher with a better understanding of the data.

Now, let's take a look at some of the more widely used measures of variability.

Variability and Variation

Let's consider the following scenario:

> Two teachers are comparing notes after a semester has concluded. They have taught different sections of the same subject, using the same teaching approach and the same exams. In the course of their discussions, they have discovered that the average grade for each of the two sections was 81. One teacher felt that it had been a wonderful year with the students proceeding at a similar pace. The second teacher, however, indicated that the semester had been difficult because the class had several talented students who grasped the subject extremely well and several slow learning pupils who did comparatively poor work. Obviously, the average grade for the two classes didn't reveal the entire story. In the first case, the pupils were closely grouped around the 81 average, a fairly homogeneous group of students, with few low and few high scores. In the second class, the pupils had a wide range of abilities, a heterogeneous group, with some scores in the 60s and some in the 90s.

It should be clear from this scenario that averages alone don't properly describe the situation with respect to the grades. To rectify this situation, let's consider four measures of variability: the range, interquartile range, average deviation, and standard deviation. **Each of these measures can be associated only with variables.**

Range

Here's a simple measure of variability, the difference between the largest and the smallest value in the set of observations. At times, this summary measure, referred to as the range, is reported by indicating the lowest and then the highest value. To illustrate, consider the six observations on years of tenure, given in Exhibit 6.1. The range can be reported as being from 2 to 8 years or as 6 years. It seems more logical and descriptive to express the range as being from 2 to 8 years. This gives the person analyzing the data a clearer picture of where the observations lie.

For our 2SCH4 database in Appendix E, considering the SAT Verbal Score , the range is presented as 460 or from 220 to 680. As will be true for all summary measures, an individual value may not be meaningful until it is compared with the corresponding summary measure from another data set.

A caution in using the range: it is strongly influenced by a single extreme observation. To illustrate, consider the six years of tenure observations:

$$2 \quad 3 \quad 5 \quad 6 \quad 6 \quad 8$$

where the range is from 2 to 8, clearly 6 years. Suppose there had been a single teacher in the group with 20 years of tenure. Now the range becomes 18 or from 2 to 20. You can see how this single value gives a distorted picture of the dispersion of the observations.

Inter-Quartile Range

As a partial effort to diminish the possible influence of extreme data points, the inter-quartile range describes the range within which the middle 50% of the observations lie when the data have been ranked or ordered. It is important that the data be ranked or ordered for the inter-quartile range to have any meaning.

For our example with six teachers, it doesn't make sense to divide the group into four sub-groups of 25% each. For the 2SCH4 data set in Appendix E, however, it does make sense. For this set of 224 observations, the inter-quartile range is reported . as being from 350 (referred to as the **first quartile** (*) or Q1) to 500 (referred to as the **3rd quartile** (*) or Q3). Frequently, the inter-quartile range is reported as the difference between the two quartiles or, in this case, 150. Again, an objection to reporting just the 150 is that it doesn't give the analyst a picture of where this middle 50% of the observations lie.

While it is generally agreed that the inter-quartile range is a better measure of variability than the range, it still has a major deficiency which is that it does not take into consideration all of the observations in the data set. To overcome this inadequacy the next measure of variability, the average deviation, is introduced.

Average Deviation

In analyzing a specific variable for a set of AUs, it should be clear that not all the observations will be the same. Therefore, it seems appropriate to examine the extent to which individual observations vary, or deviate, from some central point, usually taken as the arithmetic mean.

Consider the illustration in Exhibit 6.1 of the six teachers where the variable being studied is years of tenure. The first teacher's value indicated in the example is 6 years. Since the average for the group is 5 years, this teacher's observed years of tenure deviates or differs from the average by+1 year (6–5). The second teacher in the example has 3 years of tenure. This individual deviates from the average of the group by–2 years (3–5). These individual differences, +1 and –2, are referred to as deviations from the mean. The+value indicates an observation greater than the mean and a-value indicates an observation less than the mean.

In the column labeled $(X - \overline{X}) = x$ (column 2), each of the deviations from the arithmetic mean is presented. The use of the smallx, as contrasted with the large X, is standard in the field of statistics. A largexrepresents an individual value of a variable and a small x represents the deviation or difference between an individual value and the average for the group. Note that the values sum to 0 , which should always be the case except for possible minor differences due to rounding. Column (3), on the other hand indicates the amount of the deviation (difference) but not the direction. Notice that the minus signs are missing. These differences are referred to as absolute deviations (Note the use of the vertical signs around the $| X - \overline{X} |$ term. These symbols are referred to as absolute value symbols. This helps differentiate the term from $(X - \overline{X})$, for example.)

It should be evident that the sum of these absolute deviations represents the total amount by which the individual six years of tenure observations differ from the arithmetic mean. Since this sum represents the total amount of the deviations from the arithmetic mean, why can't we obtain an average amount of the deviations by dividing by the number of observations, in this case 6 ? So, this operation yields:

$$\Sigma | X - \overline{X} | / n = 10/6 = 1.67$$

which we will call the average deviation about (or from) the arithmetic mean. (Recall from Appendix D that the S is a summation sign and indicates that an addition is required.) It is generally understood that the phrase average deviation refers to this measure of variation.

As stated earlier, the average deviation of 1.67 by itself may have little meaning, but when compared to the corresponding average deviation for a similar group one can begin to get a feel for the difference in variation between the two groups.

Although the average deviation is fairly easy to understand, it is not widely used in educational research and evaluation. Consider, next, the standard deviation which is fundamental to assessing differences in variability and vital to inferential statistics, the topic to be considered in Chapter 7.

Standard Deviation

The standard deviation and its square, the **variance** (*), are by far the most important measures of variation or dispersion, particularly when inferences are to be made from a sample to a population. Slightly more difficult to calculate than the average deviation, the standard deviation is quite similar to the average deviation. All observations are taken into consideration and deviations are, again, measured from the average. It varies less from sample to sample drawn from the same population than any other measure of variation. It is more stable; and, therefore, in sampling it yields a more accurate estimate of the dispersion in the population from which the sample(s) is being selected.

The symbol for the standard deviation in a sample is the letter S. The corresponding symbol in the population from which the sample has been drawn is the small Greek letter sigma, σ . Like the average deviation, the standard deviation is also an average of deviations from the arithmetic mean. The major difference is that the deviations are squared, totaled, averaged, and then the square root is taken to get the measure back to the original units (in our first example tenure, not tenure-squared).

Let's walk through the process using the example of years of tenure in Exhibit 6.1. Indicated below are the steps which are followed in computing the standard deviation. Relax! The recipe you are now given is for illustrative purposes only. We'll let the PC or the MAC do all the work for us after this illustration. Consider formula (6.1), which is the usual expression for the standard deviation. The five steps which follow are keyed to formula (6.1) and the data in Exhibit 6.1. Here we go:

$$S = \sqrt{\sum (X - \overline{X})^2 / n} \qquad\qquad (6.1)$$

$$= \sqrt{24 / 6} = \sqrt{4} = 2 \text{ years of tenure}$$

1. The arithmetic mean is calculated; in this case it is seen to be 5 years of tenure.

2. The arithmetic mean is subtracted from each observation, namely, $(X - \overline{X})$ (column 2 in the example). Recall that the total of this column should be 0.

3. The next step, and a new one, is to square these deviations from the arithmetic mean, as is indicated in column 4, where the total is seen to be 24.

4. This sum of the squared deviations is then averaged by dividing by the sample size, namely, n. (Note: some texts divide by (n–1). This difference will be described briefly in Chapter 7.) For this example, the average of the sum of the squared deviations is seen to be 24/6 = 4.

5. The final step is to take the square root of this average. For this example it follows that the result is $\sqrt{4}=2$. This number, 2, is reported as the standard deviation of the six observations and is expressed in years of tenure.

Not to fret!! For future calculations and analyses, the PC will do the work for us.

Suppose that in analyzing another group of, say, 10 teachers, it was observed that the standard deviation was 4 years of tenure. What would this mean when comparing this second group with the first group of 6 teachers? At this stage in our travels through descriptive statistics, all we could say is that the second group appears to have greater variability than the first group. More on this as we progress through this manual.

Now, let's look at the data for 2SCH4 in Appendix E. For the set of 224 SAT Verbal Scores , the standard deviation is reported as 101.1. This number represents the variability in the 224 SAT Verbal Scores around the arithmetic mean. If we had another set of SAT Verbal Scores, say, from another school and the standard deviation was calculated as 50.7, we would be able to conclude that this second group appears to be considerably more homogeneous (less variability around the average) than the first group. The first group, conversely, can be considered more heterogeneous with respect to its SAT Verbal Scores. (Note: it would not be appropriate to state that the first group has approximately twice as much variability as the second.) The main thing to remember here is that a standard deviation in and of itself does not necessarily give us useful information. It is essential that we have something with which to compare the calculated standard deviation, usually another group of AUs.

Now let's move on to another set of descriptive measures; these we will refer to as positional.

Positional

Up to this point, in describing a set of data with measures of central tendency and measures of variability, we have not really considered questions such as: Where does a score of 85 stand within the group of scores? Is it above or below average, and how far? The family of measures which will help us to answer these questions is referred to in this manual as positional.

A positional measure, when associated with an actual value for a variable, gives information on where the value lies within the group (i.e., it positions the specific value). Although there are many such measures, this manual addresses only two: percentiles and Z scores.

Percentiles

It should be fairly clear that a "raw" or actual score (value of the variable of interest) does not describe where the value lies, only what the value is. When a score is converted to a percentile, the resulting numerical quantity (the percentile) indicates the percentage of the observations in the group which is less than the given score. For example, if a raw score of 86 has associated with it the percentile of 95, this means that 95% of the observations in the data set have values less than the raw score of 86. The actual calculation for percentiles is fairly straightforward but somewhat tedious. Fortunately, most statistical software packages are set up to provide several basic percentiles and to allow for the calculation of others. So, in this manual the actual calculation process is not described.

Consider the 2SCH4 database in Appendix E and the variable SAT Verbal Score on. We have already examined three percentiles without explicitly indicating so, namely, the 25th, 50th and 75th percentiles. Recall that the median score was 430. This would correspond to the 50th percentile, since 50% of the observations are above and 50% below this value.

When the inter-quartile range was discussed, it was indicated that this range included the middle 50% of the observations. Therefore, 25% must be excluded at the bottom end of the scores and also at the top end of the scores. Hence, the lower score for the interquartile range, namely, 350 must correspond to the 25th percentile, since 25% of the observations are less than this score. On the other hand, the upper score for the inter-quartile range was reported as 500 which must correspond to the 75th percentile since 25% of the scores are above this value. Piece of cake!?

Now, let's look at two other percentiles indicated in Appendix E for 2SCH4 :

1. An SAT Verbal Score of 560 is indicated as the 90th percentile. Therefore, 90% of the observations are less than this score.

2. At the other extreme, a score of 290 is reported as the 10th percentile which means 10% of the observations are less than this score.

Percentiles serve many uses, three of which are:

1. To convert a raw score on a test to indicate where the raw score is positioned with respect to some national norm or standard (frequently reported on standardized tests).

2. To convert a raw score on a test to indicate where the raw score is positioned spect to a given group (such as the students within a given institution).

3. To convert raw scores for comparative purposes across years or across groups within, say, the same organization.

Now, let's take a look at a second positional measure, the Z score (sometimes referred to as a standard score).

Standard Score: Z Score

To calculate a **Z score** (*), unlike the percentile, information on both the average and the standard deviation within a group is needed. Let's consider the example in Exhibit 6.1, where the mean is reported as 5 and the standard deviation as 2. Suppose we ask the question "Where is an individual with 8 years of tenure positioned? What are the steps we might follow to respond to this question?

1. An individual with 8 years of tenure is certainly above average for the group.

2. This individual is actually 3 years above the average years of tenure (8–5 = 3).

3. How might we express these 3 years in terms of number of standard deviations? Recall that the standard deviation for this data is 2. Clearly, 3 is 1.5 standard deviations above average (3/2 = 1.5).

Believe it or not, this 1.5 corresponds to the Z score associated with an observed value of 8 years of tenure when comparing this individual to his/her own group. This suggests a possible formula for calculating a Z-score, namely,

$$Z = (X - \overline{X}) / S \qquad\qquad (6.2)$$

Recall that S is the standard deviation. Now, what about a person whose years of tenure is 2 ? Recall that the average is 5 and the standard deviation is 2. Let's follow the same logic as above.

1. An individual with 2 years of tenure is certainly below the average for the group.

2. 2 years of tenure is 3 years below the average for the group. This might also be expressed as being-3 years away from the average when compared with the group average.

3. This-3 years can be seen to be 1.5 standard deviations below average [(2–5)/2]. So, let's say that the Z score corresponding to 2 years of tenure is-1.5.

So, the process really is quite simple. Let's repeat the steps to convert an original value of a variable to a Z-score:

1. The original value, say X, is subtracted from the average for the group.

2. This difference, which may be positive (greater than the average) or negative (less than the average) is then divided by the standard deviation for the group.

3. The resulting number (positive or negative) is the Z score and represents the number of standard deviations the actual observation is above (positive) or below (negative) the average for the group.

Hence, using a standard score makes it possible to identify:

1. Where the original value is positioned within the group in terms of numbers of standard deviations.

2. Where the original value is positioned with respect to some larger group (say a norm group) with respect to numbers of standard deviations.

There are other standard scores, such as T-scores, Normal Curve Equivalents (NCE) and Stanines, which are not considered in this manual but can be found in any text on tests and measurement. (Please see the References.)

For a large group of teachers in which years of tenure is again the variable of interest Exhibit 6.2 presents a graphic comparison between original scores and the corresponding Z-scores. The arithmetic mean is 12 and the standard deviation is 4. Also in the exhibit is the corresponding Z-score scale.

Relational

Up to this point in our journey through descriptive statistics we have been examining only a single characteristic at a time. Consider the following situations:

1. Describe the distribution of achievement test scores for a given group of subjects.

2. For a group of nurses, describe the amount of variability in their scores on a test assessing their abilities to perform certain basic nursing operations.

3. Describe the proportion of registered voters who would support a given issue if they were to vote today.

Each of these situations considers a single characteristic only. Frequently, however, a researcher or analyst is concerned with analyzing the possible relationship or association among two or more characteristics. Consider the following questions:

1. Is there a relationship between a teacher's years of tenure and annual contract salary? (We would certainly hope so!)

2. Can we conclude that scores on a given aptitude test can be used to predict achievement scores in the same subject?

3. Is it possible that high school grade point average could be used to predict what score an individual might make on the verbal Scholastic Aptitude Test?

4. Is it conceivable that the high school grade point average, SAT test scores (both verbal and math) and a value of a socio-economic variable might be useful in predicting success or failure (perhaps as measured by the grade point average at the end of the senior year of college) for a prospective college student?

The answers to these four questions clearly involve more than one characteristic. The reader should note that the first three questions above involve two variables. We refer to this situation as the bivariate (two variable) case. The fourth question involves more than two variables, namely, high school grade point average, SAT verbal and SAT math scores, the value of some socio-economic index or variable, and the final grade point average upon graduation from college. This situation we refer to as multivariate (more than two variables).

Regardless of whether we are dealing with the bivariate or multivariate situation, we are examining possible relationships among two or more characteristics. The reader should note that the above examples all deal with variables rather than attributes. **The discussions which follow in this chapter will deal with relationships among variables only.**

Two Variables

Two variables are said to be related, or correlated, if there seems to be a fairly consistent pattern relating one variable to the other. Specifically, high teacher salaries (one variable) tend to be associated with more years of experience (a second variable). Higher scores on aptitude tests (one variable) tend to be associated with higher scores on achievement tests (a second variable).

Consider Exhibit 6.3. In this exhibit there are six different figures, A through F. Let's recall a few things about graphic presentations. The left hand corner of the graph is referred to as the origin and represents starting points, or zero (0) values, for both the vertical scale (referred to as the Y axis or the **ordinate** (*)) and the horizontal scale (referred to as thexaxis or the **abscissa** (*)). If we assume that these two axes represent scales for two variables, then moving up the vertical axis from the origin provides increasing values for the Y variable and moving to the right from the origin on thexaxis also represents increasing values for thexvariable.

At the top of each figure is an indication of a numerical value for something called r . We'll weave the interpretation of this r value into the discussions which follow.

Now, let's examine each of the six figures and see what kind of a visual interpretation we can draw:

1. Figure A: Note that as values ofx(the horizontal scale) increase so do values of Y (the vertical scale). Note also that if we were to fit a straight line to the plotted points, all points would appear on the line. We shall refer to this situation as being a perfect positive correlation or relationship. (Note that here r = +1.)

2. Figure B: This figure looks a lot like Figure A except an inverse relationship appears to exist. Asxincreases, the Y values appear to decrease. Once again, if we were to fit a straight line to this figure, all the points would be on that line. This we refer to as a perfect negative relationship or correlation. (Note that here r = –1.)

3. Figure C: In this figure, it should be apparent that no matter what the value for xmight be, Y assumes only one of two values. It would be safe to say that there is no relationship betweenxand Y. (Note that here r = 0.)

4. Figures D, E, and F: As our eyes move from Figure D to E to F, it seems that there is more scatter on the plots. Figure D plots are closer to a straight line than Figure E. Figure F, on the other hand, has plots which appear further from a straight line. (Note that the values for r move from .92 through .91 to .54. This movement from a value near +1 towards a value of 0, reflects the decrease in the positive relationship.)

Now, let's consider another set of data, this time for 10 students studying a curriculum in social work. The scores of these 10 students on hypothetical exams appear in Exhibit 6.4. Scores are given for social psychology, counseling, government/law, and sociology. Figure A suggests that counseling scores bear a perfect positive relationship (r = +1) with social psychology scores while Figure B suggests a perfect negative relationship (r = –1) between counseling scores and government/law scores. (You can conjecture what this might mean in the real world!) It also appears (Figure C) that there is little, if any relationship (an r value close to 0) between the sociology scores and the counseling scores.

It is appropriate now to consider several statistical definitions and terms which will be necessary as we move further into the correlation and regression analyses. First of all, the distinction between correlation and regression:

> Correlation involves examining the possible relationship between two or more variables without any implication of cause or effect. For example, it is generally agreed that there is a high positive correlation between intelligence and aptitude test scores. Also, a recent study has shown that there is a high positive relationship between SAT verbal and SAT math scores within a given school district.

> Regression, on the other hand, generally implies some cause/effect relationship or at least the ability to use one variable as a predictor of another variable. An excellent illustration here is the use of an aptitude test score as a predictor of achievement in a given subject area.

Now, let's examine the form of a regression equation (i.e., the equation which one might use to predict the expected value of one variable from an observed value of another variable). We refer to the predicted variable as being **dependent** (*) and the predictor variable as being **independent** (*).

Consider the values for x (the independent variable) and Y (the dependent variable) in the following table.

Independent Variable	X	0	1	2	3	4	5
Dependent Variable	Y	3	5	7	9	11	13

Upon examination of the pairs of x and Y values (read vertically in the table), it should be clear (reading from left to right) that as values of x increase, so do values of Y. As a matter of fact, as x increases by 1, Y increases by 2. We can also notice that when x = 0, Y = 3. Putting this information together yields the following predicting, or regression, equation:

$$Y = 3 + 2X.$$

We refer to the value 3 as the **Y intercept** (*) and the value 2 as the **slope of the line** (*) or the **coefficient of x** (*). This line is referred to as the **regression line** (*) and is used to predict a value for Y (the dependent variable) from a value of x (the independent variable).

We can generalize by saying that the **bivariate** (*) (two variables) regression line, in general, can be expressed by the equation $Y = a + bX$, where

$$a \Rightarrow Y \text{ intercept}$$
$$b \Rightarrow \text{slope of the line or coefficient of X}$$

Any bivariate regression line can be described by the above general equation when specific values for a and b are identified. This line of regression describes a relationship between x and Y which is **linear** in nature. It is beyond the scope of this manual to discuss curvilinear relationships, but several of the references address this topic. The magic of our statistical software will take care of calculations for us later.

You may recall that we have described the degree of correlation by using the letter r. In statistical parlance, r is referred to as the **correlation coefficient** (*) or **Pearson's product–moment correlation coefficient** (*). You need not let this esoteric vocabulary disturb you. It is sufficient to recognize, as we saw in Exhibits 6.3 and 6.4, that r ranges from –1 (perfect negative correlation) through 0 (no correlation) to +1 (perfect positive correlation).

While r is an index between–1 and+1, r^2 will range from 0 to 1.00. In statistical jargon, r^2 is referred to as the **coefficient of determination** (*). This term gives us the proportion of the variability or variation in the dependent variable Y that may be accounted for by differences, or variation, in the independent variable X. The closer to 1.00, the greater the proportion of variability in Y explained by X. More on this as we proceed further in our examples.

Now, let's consider the data in Exhibit 6.5, where aptitude test scores are being compared with achievement test scores. The data represent 27 pairs of scores. It should be clear that there is a strong positive relationship and that, as aptitude scores increase, so do achievement test scores. The relationship is not perfect but, the value of $r^2 = 0.9253$ tells us that 92.53% of the variation (or differences) in achievement test scores can be accounted for by differences in aptitude scores. Conversely, only 7.47% (1.000–0.9253) of the differences in achievement scores can be accounted for by something other than the aptitude scores.

If one were to predict an expected achievement score from a given aptitude score, the regression equation would be

$$Y' = 24.92 + 0.734 \, X.$$

That is, multiplying the aptitude score by 0.734 and then adding the result to 24.92 would yield an expected achievement score. There is clearly some error in this prediction since all of the plotted points are not on the straight line. The reader should notice that a Y' is being used in this regression equation. From here forward, we will be using the letter Y to represent actual values and the symbol Y' to represent the predicted expected value. This regression equation could be calculated using available statistical software, such as NCSS, Statview, or SPSS, as referred to earlier in this manual.

Now, let's examine Exhibit 6.6 in which it is again clear that there is a positive relationship between the two variables. However, even though the regression equation could be used to make a prediction, we do notice that there appears to be some nonrandom variability of the plotted points about the straight line. If the straight line were not in the graph, one might conclude that some form of curve describes the relationship quite well. The reader is urged to plot his or her data so that nonrandom behavior of the plotted points becomes evident. The message here is that a straight line might well do the job in predicting, but some other line or curve might be better.

Now, let's take a look at Exhibit 6.7, in which a blind use of computer software would yield a correlation of 0 (i.e., r = 0). However, a visual examination of the data plots suggests that there might, in fact, be two relationships between X and Y. If we ignore the points associated with an x value of 17 and Y values of 4, 5, and 6, the first nine points seem to indicate a negative relationship, while the last nine points indicate a positive relationship. In cases like this, it is possible that there may be two different sets of x and Y values (i.e., two different populations). So, the r = 0 would be misleading and possibly illogical. The message here, again, is to examine the plotted points and to know your data well.

In Exhibit 6.8, blind use of statistical software would yield a positive relationship between X and Y , with the regression line being given as Y' = 3.1+0.617 X. If the single regression line were not evident in the graph, one might review the data and suspect that there may be a negative relationship between x and Y. This is illustrated by the regression equation given for the four points in the lower left of the graph, where the regression equation is Y' = 8.2–0.8 X. The message, once again, is to be sure to view the graphic relationship between x and Y before drawing any potentially dangerous and erroneous conclusions.

The reader also needs to be aware that extreme values (sometimes referred to as outliers) can distort the value for the correlation coefficient, as well as the regression line. In Exhibit 6.9, this situation is illustrated. The first four points in the lower left of the graph indicate a perfect negative correlation (because the points would lie on a straight line if the line were plotted). The addition of the point represented by X and Y both equaling 5 would yield a calculated correlation coefficient of 0 . And adding the other two points to the right in the graph would change the computed value of r from 0 to 0.923 and then to 0.978. The message here is that extremes can distort and give a false picture of relationships between two variables. Again, knowing your data is essential.

Exhibit 6.10 presents data for 10 students. One characteristic is clearly a variable, semester average. The other, a cooperativeness measure, is clearly a rank. While analyzing the data assuming both characteristics were variables would yield numerical results, it would be appropriate to convert the semester average to a ranking also and then to use some ranking methodology, such as **Spearman's rho** (*), to determine the degree of the relationship between the two characteristics. It is important to note that, even though many statistical software programs will calculate regression equations regardless of whether the characteristics are variables or attributes, it is essential to have variables to estimate regression lines and correlation coefficients. There are, however, techniques using dummy variables (from attributes) which allow the researchers to introduce attributes into regression analyses. (Please see references.)

The material which follows uses the two databases in Appendices E and F to examine correlation and regression analyses.

2SCH4 DATABASE

As has been previously indicated, the 2SCH4 database consists of records for 224 students. Information and statistical output for this database appear in Appendix E. It might be of interest to see whether the SAT Verbal score (the dependent variable, Y) is related to the high school grade point average (GPA), the independent variable. The scatter plot suggests a weak positive relationship, with the regression equation being given as:

$$Y' = 146.9 + 94.3 X$$

An increase in GPA of **.1** would result in a predicted average increase in SAT verbal of 9.4 points (.1x94.3 = 9.4). Predicted SAT verbal scores for five GPAs follow:

High school GPA	1.5	2.0	2.5	3.0	3.5
SAT verbal score	288.4	335.5	382.7	429.8	477.0

A comparison of the predicted SAT verbal scores with the basic data or the graph in Appendix E, supports the fact that there is great variability in the data when studying the relationship between these two variables. Note that r = .4640. It follows that the coefficient of determination is given as $r^2 = .2153$. This means that only 21.53% of the variability (or differences) in the SAT verbal scores can be accounted for (or explained by) differences in the high school GPAs. Therefore, 78.47% (1.00–2153) of the variability in the SAT verbal scores remains unexplained by the high school GPAs. This suggests a need to look for other possibly contributing characteristics.

ENGSCO DATABASE

In Appendix F is presented a set of printouts for a database called ENGSCO. This database consists of four variables for 45 students. These variables are Freshman marks (at the end of the freshman year), a CAT score (a version of an aptitude test score), high school GPA, and an English pre–test score.

Descriptive statistics (means and standard deviations) for each variable appear in Appendix F, as well as the correlations (r values) between all six possible pairwise comparisons. A scatter plot is given in which high school GPA is used as the independent variable to predict final college freshman marks. An examination of this scatter plot suggests a positive relationship but with some variability. The regression equation is seen to be:

$$Y' = 21.59 + 20.0 \ X$$

with the correlation coefficient, r, being .669 . From this information, the coefficient of determination, r^2, is seen to be 4476, indicating that 44.76% of the variability in the college freshman marks can be accounted for by differences in the high school GPA.

The regression equation indicates that an increase in high school GPA of .1, for example, would result in a predicted expected increase of 2.0 in the freshman marks (.1*20.0). (Please note that the symbol* is frequently used to represent a multiplication.)

High school GPA	1.5	2.0	2.5	3.0	3.5
Freshman marks	51.6	61.6	71.6	81.6	91.6

In comparing these predicted values with what the data and graph indicate, it is clear that there is a great deal of variability associated with the prediction process. Chapter 7 deals with the issues associated with precision or accuracy of the predictions.

More Than Two Variables

We have just completed our review of the two–variable (bivariate) situation, when considering both correlation (*Is there a relationship?*) and regression (*Can I use one variable to predict another?*). The next step in studying relationships among variables is to look at the situation when we have more than two variables (the multivariate case), still retaining a single dependent variable (DV) but allowing our analysis to consider more than one independent variable (IV).

Before looking at 2SCH4 and ENGSCO, let's consider the following illustration. Assume that the AU is a public school teacher within some given school district. Assume further that there are four variables of interest in our analysis, with the dependent variable being annual contract salary in $1,000's. Indicated below are the symbols associated with the four variables:

Y = annual contract salary in $1,000

X_1 = years of tenure

X_2 = semester credits in college

X_3 = average schedule contract salary in $1,000 for teachers in the same schedule as the specific AU

A multiple regression equation, analogous to the bivariate regression we just studied, might be represented by the following equation:

$$Y' = a + b_1 X_1 + b_2 X_2 + b_3 X_3$$

where a again represents the Y intercept value and the coefficients for the Xs are analogous to the slope which we encountered as the numerical value for b in the bivariate case. Since the coefficient, b_1, is associated with years of tenure, it indicates the amount of change in expected annual contract salary for each additional year of tenure, when the other two variables, X_2 and X_3, are held constant.

Now, let's examine the two databases which we used in our development of the descriptive statistics for bivariate regression, namely, ENGSCO and 2SCH4.

ENGSCO DATABASE

As you may recall, the ENGSCO database consists of observations on 45 students. The four variables in the study are college freshman marks (at the end of the freshman year), a CAT score, high school GPA, and a college English pre–test score. In our bivariate analyses, we found that the regression equation relating final freshman marks (the dependent variable or Y) to high school GPA (the independent variable or X) was given by:

$$Y' = 21.59 + 20.0 X$$

The correlation coefficient and coefficient of determination were, respectively, .669 and .4476.

Let's assume that it is of interest to describe the relationship between final freshman marks (Y) and the three other variables in the data base. In a sense, then, we are going to develop (rather the PC is going to develop) estimates for the regression equation in which there are to be three IVs and the single DV. The regression equation which provides the best fit to the data, referred to in the field of statistics as the line of **least squares** (*), can be found in the printout in Appendix F , namely,

$$Y' = 21.6 + .0032 X_1 + 15.8 X_2 + .52 X_3$$

where the coefficients of the three IVs indicate the extent to which each IV enters into the prediction of the final freshman mark. To illustrate, when considering the CAT score (X_1), for each point change in the CAT the final freshman mark is expected to change by .0032 points. The reader should note that the value for b_1 is given in Appendix F as .3241E–02. This is a scientific notation which is used in some statistical software. The –02 (following the letter E, which stands for exponent) means to move the decimal point two places to the left of the number .3241, resulting in the value .003241. If the slope were negative, there would be a minus sign in front of the numbers. This is clearly not a very strong variable for prediction purposes since to increase the expected final freshman mark by 3 points would require an increase in the CAT of 1,000 points (1,000*.0032 = 3.2), where the * is a symbol meaning multiply. This is obviously not a very likely change in CAT when you consider the range of CAT scores in the ENGSCO database. From the printouts in Appendix F, it is seen that the over–all coefficient of determination is .4986 .

Now, let's suppose we decide to throw out the CAT as a predictor because it doesn't look very good and recalculate the regression equation using only high school GPA and the college English pre–test scores as predictors (Page F.5). The resulting multiple regression equation becomes:

$$Y' = 21.8 + 15.8 X_2 + .52 X_3$$

with a coefficient of determination equal to .4986 .

By this time you are probably confused by all this discussion about a bivariate relationship and two different multiple regressions. It might help to look at a table (sometimes referred to as a **matrix** (*)) of the bivariate correlations between each of the four variables in ENGSCO, considering all possible pairs of correlations. (These correlations are taken from the printout from the ENGSCO database in Appendix F):

	CAT	HS GPA	ENG-PRE	FRESHMARKS
CAT	1.0000	0.4329	0.5056	**0.3659**
HS GPA	0.4329	1.0000	0.5270	0.6692
ENG-PRE	0.5056	0.5270	1.0000	0.5441
FRESHMARKS	0.3659	**0.6692**	0.5441	1.0000

The four 1.0000 values along the main diagonal represent the correlations of each variable with itself (certainly a logical value). The other correlation coefficients represent the correlations between the variable name in a given column with the variable name in a given row. For example, the boxed correlation of 0.6692 is the correlation between the freshman final marks and the high school GPA.

It should be clear from the correlations in the above table that the weakest correlation, also boxed in the table above, is between the CAT and the freshman final marks, namely, 0.3659. This is certainly consistent with our observations when we calculated the multiple regression equation using all four variables. The CAT score appeared to contribute little in the way of predicting the expected freshman final marks.

Now, lets look at a table summarizing the three regression equations which we have observed for the ENGSCO database.

FRESHMAN MARKS		CAT	HS_GPA	ENG-PRE	R^2
(1) Y' =	21.59		$+20.0\,X_2$		.4479
(2) Y' =	21.60	$+.0032\,X_1$	$+15.8\,X_2$	$+.52\,X_3$.	4986
(3) Y' =	21.80		$+15.8\,X_2$	$+.52\,X_3$	.4986

From the data in the above table it can be seen that high school GPA accounts for 44.79% of the variability in the expected value of final freshman marks (regression (1) above). When all three IVs (regression (2) above) are introduced, this multiple coefficient of determination jumps to 49.86%, or an increase of 5.07% in the explained variation. Note also that, when the CAT score is dropped from the calculations, the resulting regression equation ((3) above) remains effectively the same as when the CAT score was included, and the resulting multiple coefficient of determination does not change.

Conclusion: the CAT score does not contribute any new information in predicting final freshman marks that is not already contained in the high school GPA and the college freshman pre–test score.

In Chapter 7 we will again examine this database but with the intent of making generalizations from this set of 45 students to a presumed larger population of students.

2SCH4 DATABASE

Earlier in this chapter we examined the possible relationship between SAT verbal scores (the dependent variable, Y) and high school grade point average (the independent variable, X). The calculated regression equation was given as

$$Y' = 146.9 + 94.3\, X$$

with an associated coefficient of determination (r^2) of 0.2157, indicating that 21.57% of the variation in the SAT verbal scores could be accounted for by the variation in the high school GPAs. Suppose we now introduce two other possible independent variables, namely, number of times taking the SAT and the number of (adjusted) honors level English courses taken. (Adjusted honors level courses are obtained by adding 1 to the actual number of honors level courses taken.) In the 2SCH4 database, the four variables of interest are:

Y   SAT verbal score (column 6 in the database)

X_{10} high school grade point average (column 10 in the database)

X_{12} number of honors level English courses taken (column 12 in the database)

X_5 number of times taking the SAT (column 5 in the database)

If we allow our statistical software to calculate the best fitting multiple regression line using the above four variables, it is seen from the 2SCH4 printouts in Appendix E that this line is given by the equation

$$Y' = 184.4 + 49.18\, X_{10} + 40.25\, X_{12} + 3.71\, X_5$$

where the subscripts of the IVs (the Xs) correspond to the appropriate column for the variables in the database. The multiple coefficient of determination is also seen to be 0.3318. That is, 33.18% of the variation in the SAT verbal scores can be explained by the three IVs taken together.

Since we gained some interesting information in examining the correlations between all possible pairwise comparisons of the four variables in ENGSCO, let's introduce that same matrix for this database and these four variables. Recall again that the correlation coefficients which are in the body of the table which follows relate to the specific pair of variables identified by the column and row in which the correlation appears. These correlations appear on Page E.16.

	GPA X_{10}	# of Honors X_{12}	# of Times X_5	SAT Verbal X_6
GPA	1.0000	0.5360	0.2846	0.4640
# of Honors	0.5360	1.0000	0.1802	0.5363
# of Times	0.2846	0.1802	1.0000	0.1628
SAT Verbal	0.4640	0.5363	0.1628	1.0000

It should be clear from the above table that the strongest correlation is between the number of honors level English courses taken and the SAT verbal score (not too surprising!), namely, 0.5363 (a shaded box). However, the correlation between the SAT verbal and the high school GPA is about the same, namely, 0.5360. The lowest correlation (0.1628), and also in a shaded box, is between the SAT Verbal and the number of times taking the SAT. In fact, the associated coefficient of determination is only 0.0265 ($0.1628*0.1628 = .0265$); that is, 2.65% of the variability in the SAT Verbal scores can be accounted for by the variability in the number of times taking the SAT. (Recall again that the symbol* is frequently used to represent a multiplication.)

So, let's eliminate the number of times taking the SAT as an independent variable, IV, and have our software recalculate the regression equation , which can be seen to be:

$$Y' = 185.8 + 50.3\, X_{10} + 40.3\, X_{12}$$

with an associated multiple coefficient of determination of 0.3314. This certainly suggests that our decision to eliminate the number of times taking the SAT as an IV was a good one. Why, you ponder? Let's look at the following table which summarizes the three regression calculations:

SAT VERBAL			GPA	# of HONORS*	# of Times**	R^2
(1)	Y'	=	146.9 +94.3 X_{10}			0.2157
(2)	Y'	=	184.4 +49.2 X_{10}	+40.3 X_{12}	+3.71 X_5	0.3318
(3)	Y'	=	185.8 +50.3 X_{10}	+40.3 X_{12}		0.3314

number of English honors level courses taken
*** number of times taking the SAT*

Notice that in the first bivariate regression, where the GPA is the only IV, the coefficient of determination, R^2 , is seen to be 0.2157. Using the other two variables, namely, number of English honors level courses taken and number of times taking the SAT, the R^2 becomes 0.3318, or an increase of 0.1161 (0.3318–0.2157). When we eliminate the variable with the smallest correlation with the SAT verbal scores, the number of times taking the SAT, the coefficient of determination becomes 0.3314. This suggests that any information on differences in the SAT verbal contained in the X_5 variable is also contained in the other two IVs. Hence, by eliminating the number of times taking the SAT variable from the regression calculations, we have reduced the R^2 value from 0.3318 to 0.3314. So, we see that our final predicting equation (considering only the four variables in this analysis) is:

$$Y' = 185.8 + 50.32\, X_{10} + 40.3\, X_{12}$$

Now, let's see how this equation might be employed as a predictive tool. Let's assume that we have a student who has a GPA of 3.0 and has taken 2.5 honors level English courses. We would predict his or her expected SAT verbal score by substituting the values of 3.0 and 2.5 in the above equation:

$$Y' = 185.8+50.32*3.0+40.3*2.5$$
$$= 185.8+150.96+100.75$$
$$= 437.5$$

This 437.5 is the expected SAT verbal score for a student who has a GPA of 3.0 and has taken 2.5 honors level English courses.

Let's look at one further illustration. Suppose we have a student who has a GPA of 2.5 and has taken 3 honors level English courses. What might be the expected SAT verbal score? Substituting in the above regression equation yields:

$$Y' = 185.8+50.32*2.5+40.3*3$$
$$= 185.8+125.8+120.9$$
$$= 432.5$$

Hence, the student who has a GPA of 2.5 and has taken 3 honors level English courses would be expected to obtain an SAT verbal score of 432.5. Of course, not every student with the above IVs would receive the same SAT verbal score. What we obviously need is some way to predict (estimate) the expected score and then to indicate how accurate (precise) the prediction is. More on this topic in Chapter 7.

Miscellaneous Measures

As has already been pointed out, the Pearson product–moment correlation is the most widely used measure of the extent of the linear relationship between two variables. However, it cannot be used unless data for both characteristics are variables. There are times when a researcher is faced with the problem of wanting to examine the relationship between two characteristics and the data for one or both of the characteristics is not a variable. Such conditions occur quite often in educational research. When this happens, there are special coefficients similar to or approximating the Pearson correlation coefficient.

In this manual, the researcher is presented with some of these special correlation measures. Excellent references to consult for more detail are Marascuilo and Serlin (1988), Hinkle, Wiersma, and Jurs (1988), and the Sage University Series on Quantitative Applications in the Social Sciences. To assist the researcher in making an initial decision about the special measures that may be appropriate as options to the Pearson r , a brief discussion of the major alternative measures and their possible uses follows.

Suppose the investigator wishes to find the relationship between two characteristics, one of which is an attribute and can be expressed in only two categories, such as YES or NO. An attribute with only two categories or two choices is termed **dichotomous** (*) and possesses a binomial distribution. (See Chapter 5 for a more detailed discussion of the **binomial distribution** (*).) Let's assume that the other of two characteristics is a variable. The resulting correlation may be either a **biserial correlation** (*) or a **point biserial correlation** (*).

The following is an example of a biserial correlation situation. Suppose a sample of teachers is asked the question:

"If you could go back and choose your life's occupation again, would you choose teaching?"

____Yes; ____No.

Also, suppose a measure is needed of the extent to which willingness to teach again may be either positively or negatively correlated with the age of the teacher in the sample. One characteristic, *willingness to teach again*, is an attribute; the other, *age*, is a variable. Hence, a biserial correlation is an appropriate methodology.

As stated, two coefficients are available for use in such a situation: the biserial coefficient and the point biserial coefficient. Of these two alternatives, the point biserial is usually the preferred one.

In some situations, both characteristics of interest are attributes and also dichotomous, for example, two YES/NO questions on an opinion survey. The research issue might be to examine responses to the two questions to determine whether there is any relationship between these responses. Other situations in which responses might be classified as dichotomous are:

Male versus female responses to a YES/NO item.

Responses to a YES/NO item, comparing teachers with less than 10 years of tenure with teachers having 10 or more years of tenure.

Relationship between years of tenure (teachers with less than 10 versus teachers with 10 or more) and salary (teachers earning less than $25,000 with teachers earning $25,000 or more).

When data associated with each of the above examples are presented in tabular form, there will be two columns and two rows, such as in the following table:

ATTITUDE	Male	Female	Total
YES	20	25	45
NO	45	50	95
TOTALS	65	75	140

It is clear that a similar table could be established when considering YES/NO responses for teachers with less than 10 years of tenure versus those with 10 years or more of tenure. Each of these tabular displays is referred to as a "2x2" (two–by–two) or "four–fold" table. Sometimes these tables are referred to as "2x2" contingency tables or cross–tabs. (See Chapter Five.). A number of possible alternatives exist for measuring association when considering two dichotomous characteristics:

Phi Coefficient (*): An appropriate measure when both characteristics are truly dichotomous, such as YES/NO responses to a question or the classification of sex as MALE/FEMALE.

Tetrachoric Correlation Coefficient (*): May be used when both characteristics have been artificially compressed into two categories and the underlying variables are normally distributed. The example above on years of tenure and salary might fall into this category.

Contingency Coefficient (*): This measure applies to a two–by–two table as well as tables with more than two categories for the characteristics of interest. Unlike the phi and tetrachoric coefficients, this measure is not interpretable as a correlation coefficient, since its limits do not range between–1 and+1. It is related to a procedure referred to as chi–square and is discussed in more detail in Chapter 7.

EXHIBIT 6.1   AN EXAMPLE DATA SET ON
YEARS OF TENURE

X: Years of Tenure

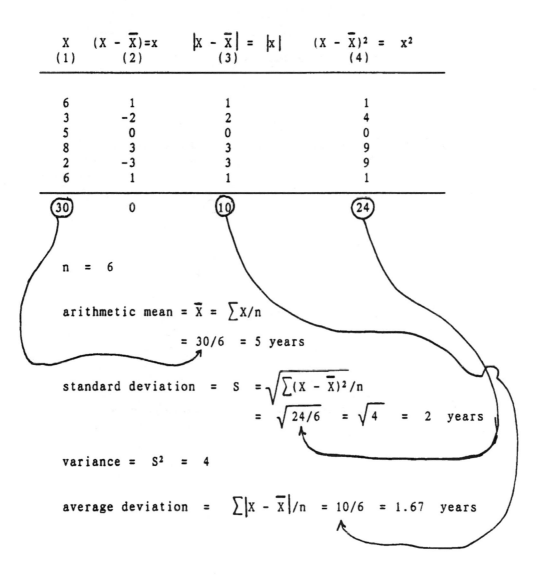

X (1)	$(X - \bar{X}) = x$ (2)	$\lvert X - \bar{X} \rvert = \lvert x \rvert$ (3)	$(X - \bar{X})^2 = x^2$ (4)
6	1	1	1
3	-2	2	4
5	0	0	0
8	3	3	9
2	-3	3	9
6	1	1	1
⃝30	0	⃝10	⃝24

$n = 6$

arithmetic mean $= \bar{X} = \sum X/n$

$\qquad = 30/6 = 5$ years

standard deviation $= S = \sqrt{\sum (X - \bar{X})^2/n}$

$\qquad\qquad = \sqrt{24/6} = \sqrt{4} = 2$ years

variance $= S^2 = 4$

average deviation $= \sum \lvert X - \bar{X} \rvert /n = 10/6 = 1.67$ years

EXHIBIT 6.2 A COMPARISON BETWEEN AN ORIGINAL VARIABLE
AND ASSOCIATED Z-SCORES

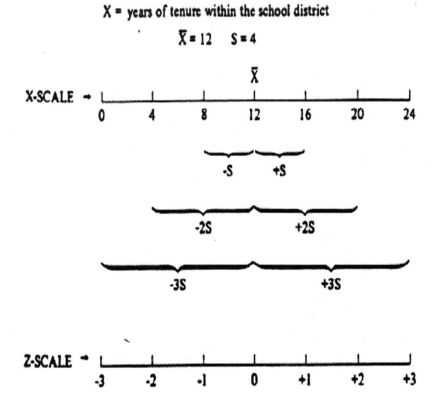

**EXHIBIT 6.3 SOME HYPOTHETICAL DATA PLOTS AND THEIR
ASSOCIATED RELATIONSHIPS (CORRELATIONS)**

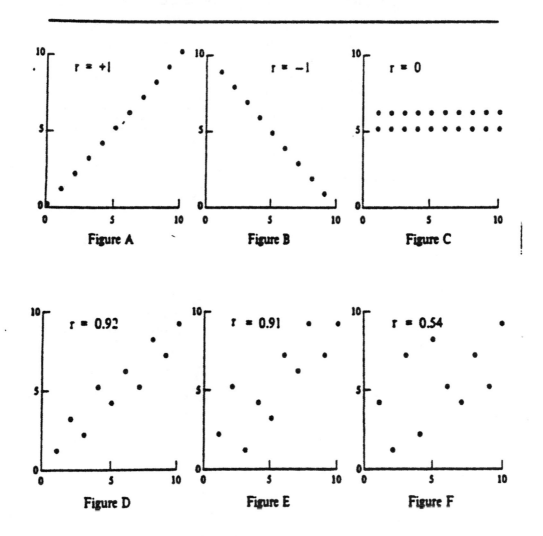

EXHIBIT 6.4 HYPOTHETICAL EXAMINATION SCORES FOR TEN STUDENTS STUDYING SOCIAL WORK

Row	Student	Social_Psych	Counseling	Govt_Law	Sociology
1	A	75	75	45	71
2	B	70	70	50	45
3	C	70	70	50	56
4	D	65	65	55	50
5	E	60	60	60	60
6	F	60	60	60	70
7	G	55	55	65	70
8	H	50	50	70	50
9	I	50	50	70	65
10	J	45	45	75	51

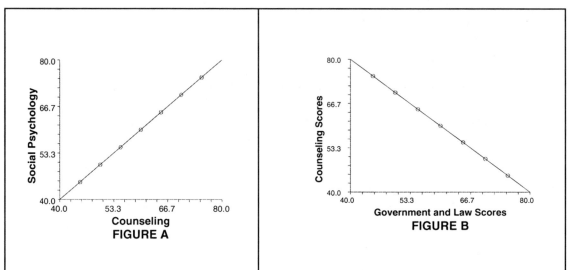

FIGURE A

FIGURE B

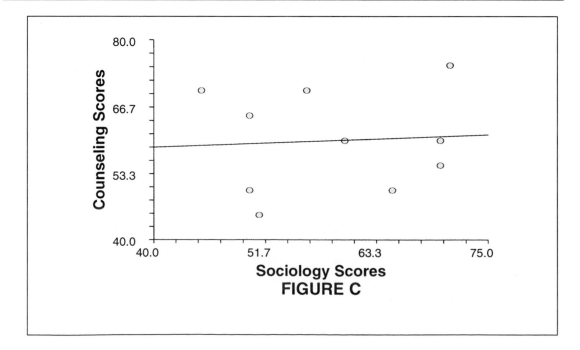

FIGURE C

EXHIBIT 6.5 A COMPARISON OF APTITUDE TEST SCORES AND ACHIEVEMENT TEST SCORES

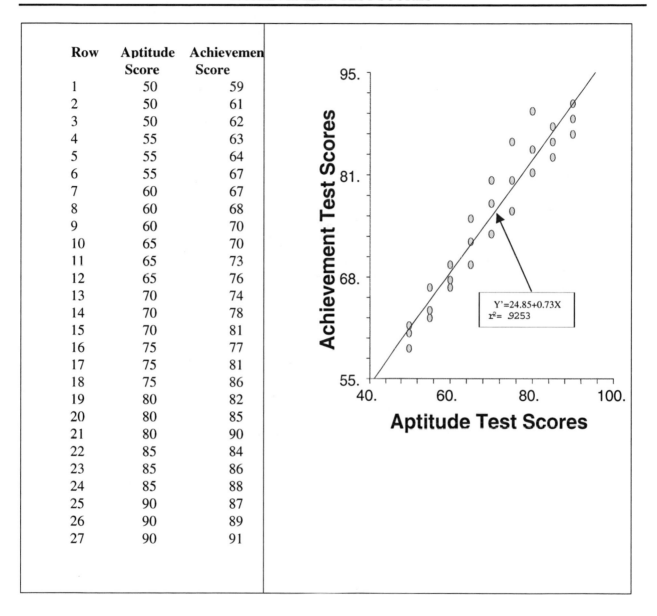

Row	Aptitude Score	Achievement Score
1	50	59
2	50	61
3	50	62
4	55	63
5	55	64
6	55	67
7	60	67
8	60	68
9	60	70
10	65	70
11	65	73
12	65	76
13	70	74
14	70	78
15	70	81
16	75	77
17	75	81
18	75	86
19	80	82
20	80	85
21	80	90
22	85	84
23	85	86
24	85	88
25	90	87
26	90	89
27	90	91

$Y' = 24.85 + 0.73X$
$r^2 = .9253$

EXHIBIT 6.6 AN HYPOTHETICAL EXAMPLE OF A DEPARTURE FROM A LINEAR REGRESSION

Row	X
1	2
2	2
3	2
4	7
5	7
6	7
7	12
8	12
9	12
10	17
11	17
12	17
13	22
14	22
15	22
16	27
17	27
18	27
19	32
20	32
21	32
22	37
23	37
24	37

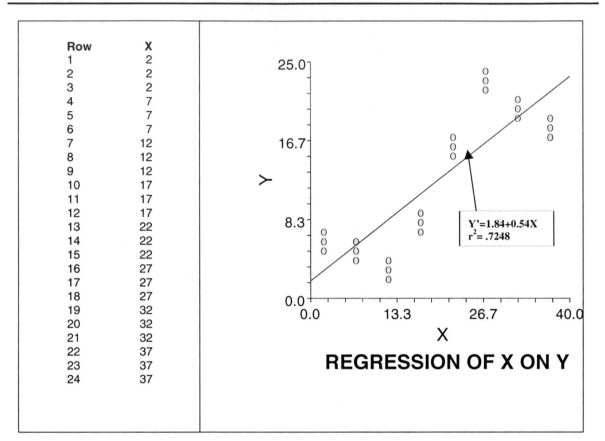

$Y'=1.84+0.54X$
$r^2= .7248$

REGRESSION OF X ON Y

EXHIBIT 6.7 ILLUSTRATING HOW A NEGATIVE AND A POSITIVE
RELATIONSHIP LOOK LIKE NO CORRELATION (r = 0)

Row	X	Y	Row	X	Y
1	2	16	12	17	6
2	2	17	13	22	8
3	2	18	14	22	9
4	7	12	15	22	10
5	7	13	16	27	12
6	7	14	17	27	13
7	12	8	18	27	14
8	12	9	19	32	16
9	12	10	20	32	17
10	17	4	21	32	18
11	17	5			

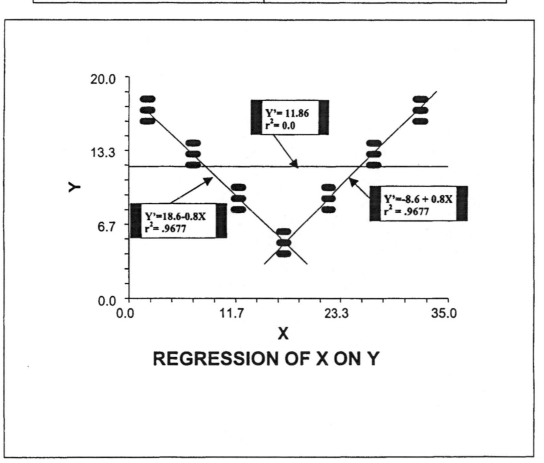

REGRESSION OF X ON Y

EXHIBIT 6.8 AN HYPOTHETICAL EXAMPLE ILLUSTRATING HOW A FAMILY OF NEGATIVE RELATIONSHIPS CAN APPEAR TO BE POSITIVE

Row	X	Y	Row	X	Y
1	2	16	12	17	6
2	2	17	13	22	8
3	2	18	14	22	9
4	7	12	15	22	10
5	7	13	16	27	12
6	7	14	17	27	13
7	12	8	18	27	14
8	12	9	19	32	16
9	12	10	20	32	17
10	17	4	21	32	18
11	17	5			

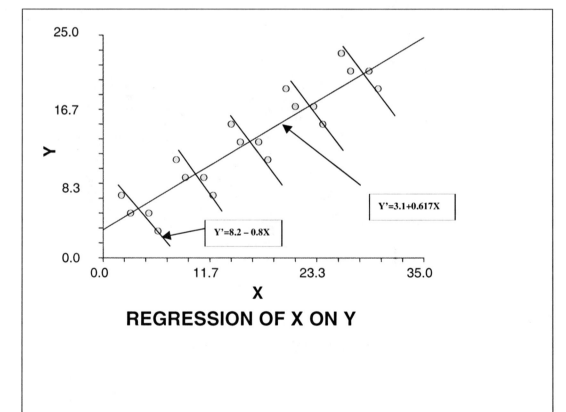

REGRESSION OF X ON Y

EXHIBIT 6.9 AN HYPOTHETICAL EXAMPLE DEMONSTRATING HOW SINGLE VALUES CAN DISTORT A RELATIONSHIP

Row	X	Y	r^2
1	1	4	
2	2	3	
3	3	2	
4	4	1	-1
5	5	5	0
6	15	15	.923
7	25	30	.978

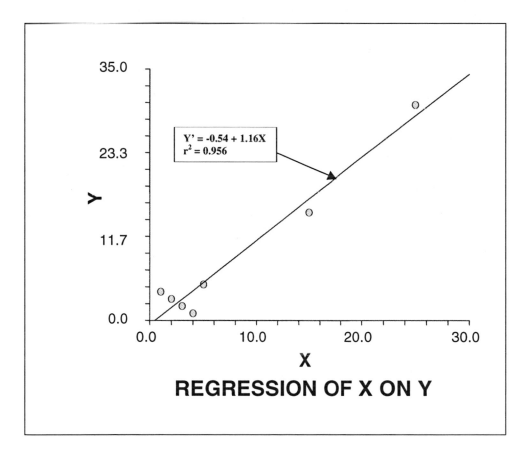

$Y' = -0.54 + 1.16X$
$r^2 = 0.956$

REGRESSION OF X ON Y

EXHIBIT 6.10 SEMESTER AVERAGES AND
COOPERATIVENESS RANKS FOR PUPILS IN A CLASS FOR GIFTED STUDENTS

Pupil	Semester Average	Cooperativeness rank (R_1)	Semester average rank (R_2)
	(1)	(2)	(3)
A	75	8	9
B	83	3	5.5
C	96	2	1
D	72	9	10
E	94	4	2
F	83	7	5.5
G	88	6	4
H	81	5	7
I	79	10	8
J	93	1	3

7. INFERENTIAL STATISTICS

In Chapter 5 the concept of distributions was introduced, looking basically at distributions associated with attributes. In Chapter 6 many of the basic elements of descriptive statistics were introduced. In this chapter the normal distribution is introduced, followed by a discussion of the critical concept of sampling distributions.

Next, the topic of statistical inference is presented, including a discussion of estimation and hypothesis testing. This is then followed by a comparison of research hypotheses, research questions, and statistical hypotheses.

The concepts of risk, confidence, and associated types of errors are presented as an introduction to specific inferential types. Finally, a series of **inferential techniques** (*) are presented in modular fashion, permitting selection of only those modules which are relevant to specific research or evaluation issues.

The Normal Probability Distribution

The concept of what is commonly referred to as the "normal probability distribution" and its theoretical graphic representation, the normal probability curve, is basic to an understanding of probability sampling. The curve of the normal distribution (sometimes called the Gaussian curve or the DeMoivre–LaPlace distribution) with its characteristic bell shape is well–known to every student of elementary statistics, as well as many in the public who have never taken a course in statistics. Properties of the normal distribution are:

1. The curve is symmetrical about its central axis (the median).

2. The values of the mean, median, and mode are equal.

3. The curve represents a specified probability distribution, i.e., the area under the curve is considered equal to one, or 100%.

The first two properties are shown in the bell–shaped graph of a normal distribution as seen in Exhibit 7.1

The third property of the normal distribution enables the researcher to make certain statements regarding the distribution of the variable represented by the curve (NOTE: only variables may be normally distributed; attributes cannot). The following points illustrate statements that can be made by using the table of normal areas as given in Appendix C.

1. Approximately 68% of the AUs fall within plus and minus one standard deviation of the mean ($\pm\sigma$).

2. Approximately 95% of the AUs will fall within plus and minus two standard deviations of the mean ($\pm2\sigma$).

3. More than 99% of the AUs will fall within plus and minus three standard deviations of the mean ($\pm3\sigma$).

EXHIBIT 7 . 1 -NORMAL PROBABILITY CURVE

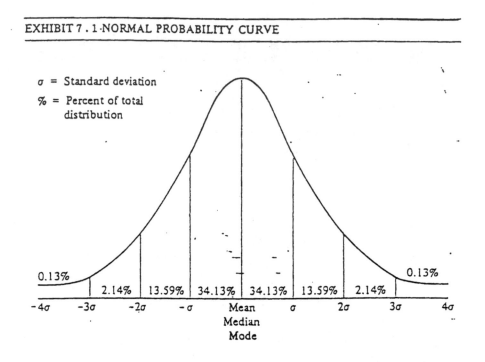

The relationship between the *standard deviation* and the percent of the observations falling within specific distances from the mean for a normally distributed variable is most important in understanding inference. So standard are these relationships that nearly every statistical text contains a table relating fractions, or multiples, of standard deviations to the proportion (percentage) of a normal distribution found within those distances of the mean. Table C.1 in Appendix C shows these relationships. In Exhibit 7.2 are excerpts from this Appendix C table. Examination of Exhibit 7.2 reveals that it is set up in terms of Z–units, or standard scores, discussed in Chapter 6.

To illustrate the use of the table and also Exhibit 7.2, recall that the raw value of a specific observation in a distribution can be transformed into a Z–score by using Formula 7.1, which is

$$Z = (X - \mu) / \sigma \qquad\qquad (7.1)$$

where

X	is the particular observation of the variable for which Z is desired.
μ	is the population mean
X–μ	is the deviation from the mean of each observation in the distribution
σ	represent the standard deviation of the variablexin the population
Z	is the relative deviation of an observation from the mean of all the observations for the variable of interest, expressed in terms of numbers of standard deviations

Suppose in a given school district the number of years of teaching experience among the instructional faculty is normally distributed. The mean number of years of experience (μ) of the faculty is 15 years and the standard deviation (σ) is 5 years. If a teacher had 24 years of teaching experience, the standard score would be:

$$Z = (X - \mu) / \sigma$$

$$= (24 - 15)/5 = 9/5 = 1.80$$

This means that the teacher's 24 years of teaching experience is 1.80 standard deviations above the mean of the population. Three questions about the teacher's experience might be of interest:

1. What percentage of the teachers in this school district are *as close or closer* to the mean of 15 years of experience as this teacher?

2. What percentage of the teachers have the *same or less* than the 24 years of experience as this teacher has?

3. What percentage of the teachers have *more than* the 24 years of experience this teacher has?

EXHIBIT 7.2 -EXCERPTS FROM APPENDIX TABLE C.1 WHICH SHOWS THE PROPORTION OF OBSERVATIONS IN A NORMAL DISTRIBUTION THAT FALL BETWEEN THE MEAN AND SPECIFIC NUMBERS OF STANDARD DEVIATIONS FROM THE MEAN

Z	0.00	0.01	0.02	0.03	0.04	0.05	0.06	
(1)	(2)	(3)	(4)	(5)	(6)	(7)	(8)	
.	.	.	.	.	.	.	..	.
1.5	0.4332	0.4345	0.4357	0.4370	0.4382	0.4394	0.4406	.
1.6	0.4452	0.4463	0.4474	0.4485	0.4495	0.4505	0.4515	.
1.7.	0.4554	0.4564	0.4573	0.4582	0.4591	0.4599	0.4608	.
← 1.8	0.4641	0.4649	0.4656	0.4664	0.4671	0.4678	0.4686	.
1.9	0.4713	0.4719	0.4726	0.4732	0.4738	0.4744	0.4750	.
.	.	.	.	.	.	.	.	.

All three questions can readily be answered by consulting Exhibit 7.2. Column 1 of the exhibit is headed "Z." In this column is seen the 1.8. indicated by an arrow. In this row in the column headed 0.00 can be read 0.4641. This number represents the proportion of the distribution between the mean and an individual observation which is 1.8 Z–units (standard deviations) above the mean (or below). The corresponding percentage is seen to be 46.41% (0.4641*100). Please see the curve which follows..

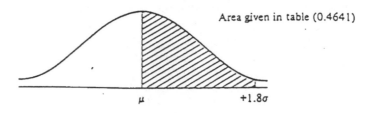

Area given in table (0.4641)

μ   +1.8σ

With the above information the three questions can be answered. The first question, reworded, was, What percent of the teachers in the school district are within plus or minus 1.80 standard deviations from the mean? The statistician refers to this as a "two–sided" or "two–tailed" situation because the researcher wishes to know the percentage of the distribution fall on *both sides* of the mean. It is a good idea in analyzing questions associated with a normal distribution to draw a simple diagram to describe the situation, as follows:

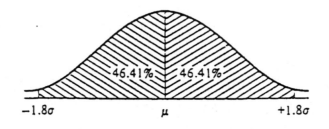

46.41%   46.41%

−1.8σ   μ   +1.8σ

Since the percentage of the distribution above and below the mean is desired, the two percentages are added to get 92.82%. This is possible because of the symmetrical property of the normal distribution. In other words, 92.82% of the teachers in this school district were within±1.8 standard deviations of the mean number of years of teaching experience. (Note that the desired percentage is shaded.)

The second question was, What percentage of the teachers have the *same or less* than 24 years of experience? The statisticians refer to this as a "one–sided" or "one–tailed" situation since it involves only the portion of the distribution falling *at or below* a certain point in the distribution. Again, drawing a simple diagram of the situation and shading in the described region, the desired percentage can be seen in the figure which follows.

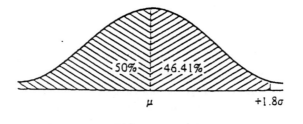

50%   46.41%

μ   +1.8σ

By substituting in Formula (7.1) it is calculated that 24 years of teaching experience in this school district has a standard score of Z = 1.80. From Exhibit 7.2 it was found that 46.41% of a normal distribution falls between the mean and 1.80 standard deviations from the mean. Because the mean and median are identical in a normal distribution, 50% of the AUs fall below the mean and 50% fall above the mean. In this situation, the 50% below the mean is added to the 46.41% above the mean to the 24 years of experience, indicating that 96.41% of the teachers in the population under study have 24 years of teaching experience or less.

The third question was, What percent of teachers have *more than* 24 years of teaching experience? This is also referred to as a "one–sided" or "one–tailed" situation because it involves only the portion of the distribution falling above a specific value. The shaded portion in the diagram which follows yields the desired percentage.

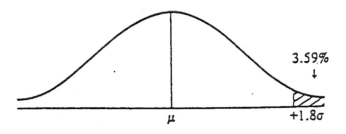

Now, how did we arrive at the 3.59%? The same logic used in answering Question 2 applies here, but now only the percentage of the distribution above 1.80 standard deviations is desired. In Question 2, it was found that 96.41% fall below+1.80 standard deviations. Therefore, subtracting the 96.41% from 100% yields 3.59% as expected to have years of teaching experience above 1.80 standard deviations, or 24 years.

It is possible to start with a percentage of area under a normal curve and then determine the corresponding Z–score, which in turn can be converted to a value of the variable of interest. For example, suppose the range that includes the middle 90% of teachers in this population is sought. The diagram for this situation might look like:

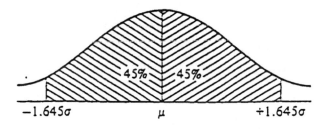

This is a "two–tailed" situation, since the percentage of teachers fall on *both sides* of the arithmetic mean is given. Therefore, 90% is divided by 2, yielding 45%, which is the percentage falling above and below the mean. Converted to a proportion, this would be .4500.

In Exhibit 7.2, the proportion 0.4500 is seen to be half way between 0.4495 and 0.4505. Therefore, the Z–score is found to be between 1.64 and 1.65, or by interpolation 1.645. If this Z–score were then to be substituted in Formula (7.2), a specific value for the variable of interest could be obtained.

$$X = \mu \pm Z*\sigma \qquad\qquad (7.2)$$

where

Z   is the standard score associated with the desired percentage. (Note that for specific "one–sided" percentages the corresponding standard score may also be found in Appendix C, Table C.2.)

μ   is the population mean

σ   represents the standard deviation of the variablexin the population

X   is the desired value for the variable in the population of interest.

Substituting in Formula (7.2) the upper limit for years of experience in the desired 90% range is seen to be:

$$X = μ + Z*σ$$

$$= 15 + 1.645*5 = 15 + 8.2 = 23.2 \text{ years}$$

Again, substituting in Formula (7.2) the lower limit of years of teaching experience within the desired 90% range can be seen to be

$$X = μ - Z*σ$$

$$= 15 - 1.645*5 = 15 - 8.2 = 6.8 \text{ years}$$

Therefore, the years of teaching experience that includes the middle 90% of the teachers in the population of interest would range from 6.8 years to 23.2 years.

The procedures for determining responses to similar questions as those posed above, but for a sample, are identical where the sample mean and standard deviation are substituted for the population mean and standard deviation.

Other types of questions which can be addressed using the normal tables in Appendix C are:

1. In terms of years of teaching experience, within what range might we find the middle 50% of teachers in this population? (Recall that this is the inter–quartile range.)

2. What percentage of the teachers have taught for less than 10 years?

3. What would be the 80th percentile for years of teaching experience?

One final point before we move ahead into a discussion of sampling distributions. There are four fairly common central percentages discussed under the assumption that the data are normally distributed. These are the middle 50%, 90%, 95%, and 99%. The table which follows relates these central percentages to the corresponding Z–scores:

CENTRAL PERCENTAGE	Z-SCORES
50%	±.6745 standard deviations
90%	±1.465 standard deviations
95%	±1.96 standard deviations
99%	±2.576 standard deviations

Information for these central percentages, as well as others, under the assumption of a normally distributed variable may be found in Table C.2 in Appendix C.

THE PREVIOUS ANALYSES ASSUME THAT THE VARIABLE OF INTEREST IS NORMALLY DISTRIBUTED.

Sampling Distributions

Have you ever wondered how it would be possible for you to use information in a single random sample and somehow, magically, say something about the population from which that sample was drawn? Perhaps not! But, perhaps you have been a bit curious.

Consider, for example, the latest release of a poll within your state. The poll is purported to have been randomly selected and, hence, its results can be generalized to all persons in the population being sampled. Reading further on in the news release we note that 72% are reported to have indicated support for a specific issue. This process of stating percentages continues throughout the news story. Then, at the end of the article, unless space problems have caused the editor to cut these final paragraphs, or in a box elsewhere on the page, you may have noted a statement something like the following: "The percentages reported in this article can be considered to be accurate within ±5% points of the true value if all persons had been in the sample and, in addition, the reader can have 90% confidence that such statements are true." Black magic? Not at all. There is a reasonable, although somewhat complex, explanation for the 5% and 90% statements. Read On!

Let's consider three very small populations, call them A, B and C. Each population consists of 40 analysis units, in each case teachers in three different elementary schools. The three populations could just as well involve AUs in three hospitals, or three sections of the same class at an institution of higher education, or even three small churches. The analysis units might, respectively, be nurses, students, or members of the congregation. Possible variables for these three different AUs might be years of employment with the hospital, years of higher education, or number of years as a member of the congregation. Exhibit 7.3 identifies the population distributions for each of these populations.

For purposes of the discussion which follows, let's stick with the teacher being the analysis unit and the three populations being three different elementary schools. Furthermore, assume that the single characteristic being examined is the variable, *years of tenure* with the given school. Exhibit 7.3 summarizes the frequency distributions for the three schools. Note that Populations A and C are similar except the larger frequencies are at the opposite end of the possible ranges of the variable. Population B, on the other hand, has four teachers at each of the 10 possible values of the variable, values which range from 1 year to 10 years. Also indicated in the Exhibit are the population averages (means) and standard deviations.

EXHIBIT 7.3 Populations A, B, and C

YEARS OF TENURE	POPULATION A FREQUENCY	POPULATION B FREQUENCY	POPULATION C FREQUENCY
1	8	4	0
2	8	4	0
3	8	4	0
4	4	4	4
5	4	4	4
6	4	4	4
7	4	4	4
8	0	4	8
9	0	4	8
10	0	4	8
Number (n)	40	40	40
Mean	3.4	5.5	7.6
Standard deviation	1.96	2.91	1.96

Now, let's assume we are sampling from Population A and that we select a single sample of five teachers by some random process. The results of this sample might be as noted in Exhibit 7.4 in the cell labeled S1, where the observed values of the variable in Sample 1 (S1) were 4, 7, 7, 1, and 1. In addition, the sample mean and standard deviation [Using (n–1) as the divisor, rather than n; we'll discuss why later in this Chapter.] are reported.

Why does the sample mean not exactly equal the population mean? Because it's a sample! Right, because it is not the population and is based upon the random selection of only five teachers. Could we say that **CHANCE ALONE DICTATED WHICH VALUES WERE OBSERVED**, and, hence, what the sample mean and standard deviation were? Yes!

Now, follow this process by assuming that nine additional random samples are selected from this same population. Naturally, after we select a single sample of five we'll have to "return" the five teachers to the population before we select the next random sample of five. (Although not relevant to our discussion here, this is referred to as sampling with replacement.) Exhibit 7.4 indicates the values of the variable in each sample, as well as the sample mean and standard deviation.

Note once again that the values of the variable in the ten samples are not all the same, and the means and standard deviations are, for the most part, also different. Why? Because they are all random samples selected from the same population and **CHANCE ALONE HAS DICTATED WHICH VALUES WERE OBSERVED.**

Now, what does this tell us? Let's identify a few possible comments under the assumption that the sampling process is random and the samples are all the same size:

1. When repeatedly sampling from a single population, the observed values of the variable under consideration will probably differ from sample to sample;

2. The observed values for the arithmetic mean, in general, will also differ from sample to sample; and,

3. Finally, the observed values for the standard deviation, in general, will also differ from sample to sample.

Once again, what causes these differences? **CHANCE ALONE, if the sampling process has been carried out randomly.**

Now, let's assume that we have decided for some reason to average all the sample means. From Exhibit 7.4, for samples drawn from Population A, we see that this average is 3.6 (reported as Grand Mean), quite close to the population average of 3.4. Now why is this to be expected? The overall average of the 10 samples now represents 50 observations. Logic tells us that **the larger the sample size, all other things being the same, the closer the sample mean should be to the population mean**.

Exhibit 7.4: Sampling Population A				
S1	S2	S3	S4	S5
4	2	2	1	7
7	4	2	1	7
7	6	1	2	3
1	2	3	4	4
1	2	5	7	6
$\overline{X} = 4.00$	$\overline{X} = 3.20$	$\overline{X} = 2.60$	$\overline{X} = 3.00$	$\overline{X} = 5.40$
$S_x = 3.00$	$S_x = 1.79$	$S_x = 1.51$	$S_x = 2.55$	$S_x = 1.80$
S6	S7	S8	S9	S10
6	1	2	1	1
6	3	2	2	2
2	5	7	3	3
4	7	7	4	5
5	3	1	6	1
$\overline{X} = 4.60$	$\overline{X} = 3.80$	$\overline{X} = 3.80$	$\overline{X} = 3.20$	$\overline{X} = 2.40$
$S_x = 1.67$	$S_x = 2.28$	$S_x = 2.95$	$S_x = 1.92$	$S_x = 1.67$

Grand Mean: 3.60
Standard Error of the mean: 0.92
Population Mean: 3.40
Population Standard Deviation: 1.96 $N = 40$

Now, stay with me, since the sample means are different, couldn't we calculate a standard deviation for these ten sample means? Of course! From Exhibit 7.4, this value is seen to be 0.92. And, as our sample sizes get larger, we would expect that this standard deviation of the sample means would get smaller and smaller. Why? Because the sample means would be getting closer to the population mean. (By the way, in statistical jargon, this standard deviation of the sample means is referred to as the **standard error of the mean** (*).)

As a matter of fact if we know the population mean (designated by the Greek letter mu, μ) and population standard deviation (designated by the Greek letter sigma, σ), then there are two very important relationships which follow as a consequence of random sampling. These are:

1. The average of all possible sample means for samples of the same size is equal to the population mean; and,

2. The standard error of the means is equal to the population standard deviation divided by the square root of n and is given by Formula (7.3).

$$\sigma_{\bar{x}} = \sigma/(n)^{1/2} \hspace{4cm} (7.3)$$

Let's continue with our assumptions. Suppose that the population with which we are dealing **is** normally distributed. Don't laugh! We know Populations A, B and C are not normally distributed; far from it. But, let's just assume so. If this is true, then fancy statistical derivations (no need to bore you with them here) have shown that the distribution of all possible sample means [referred to as the **sampling distribution of means** (*)] drawn from a normal distribution is also normal and the standard deviation of this distribution (the standard error of the mean) is equal to the population standard deviation divided by the square root of n, formula 7.4 given above. In addition, if the sample size is large enough (generally greater than 30 but actually dependent upon the shape of the population as well), the assumption that the population is normal is not necessary for the distribution of sample means to be approximately normal. In other words, **a population of any shape will yield a distribution of sample means which is approximately normal if the sample size is large enough.**

Armed with this information, it is possible for us to give probabilities (really percentages) associated with the likelihood of observing sample means less than, greater than, or between two specific values. You may recall this discussion from your earlier exposure in this chapter to the normal distribution and its magical properties.

By the way, how many different samples of size five do you think could be selected randomly from Population A? Believe it or not, 658,008. Quite a large number.

Exhibits 7.5 and 7.6 indicate similar sampling exercises when selecting samples of size 5 from populations B and C given in Exhibit 7.3. Once again, the grand means for the 10 samples are quite close to the actual population means.

Exhibit 7.5: Sampling Population B

S1	S2	S3	S4	S5
5	2	3	8	1
3	3	7	7	8
2	4	1	3	8
6	6	4	10	3
10	6	10	5	2
$\overline{X} = 520$	$\overline{X} = 4.20$	$\overline{X} = 5.00$	$\overline{X} = 6.60$	$\overline{X} = 4.40$
$S_x = 3.10$	$S_x = 1.79$	$S_x = 3.53$	$S_x = 2.70$	$S_x = 3.36$

S6	S7	S8	S9	S10
3	1	10	10	10
10	4	7	10	7
4	8	9	1	9
3	3	5	5	6
9	3	4	3	10
$\overline{X} = 5.80$	$\overline{X} = 3.80$	$\overline{X} = 7.00$	$\overline{X} = 5.80$	$\overline{X} = 8.40$
$S_x = 3.42$	$S_x = 2.59$	$S_x = 2.55$	$S_x = 4.08$	$S_x = 1.81$

Grand Mean: 5.62
Standard Error of the mean: 1.42
Population Mean: 5.50
Population Standard Deviation: 2.91   N=40

Exhibit 7.6: Sampling Population C

S1	S2	S3	S4	S5
10	7	6	9	6
9	8	8	9	7
6	4	9	8	8
9	9	9	4	6
10	6	7	8	4
$\overline{X} = 8.80$	$\overline{X} = 6.80$	$\overline{X} = 7.80$	$\overline{X} = 7.60$	$\overline{X} = 6.20$
$S_x = 1.64$	$S_x = 1.92$	$S_x = 1.30$	$S_x = 2.10$	$S_x = 1.48$
S6	S7	S8	S9	S10
4	7	5	10	6
6	4	6	10	8
8	10	4	8	7
9	8	10	9	7
7	6	10	10	9
$\overline{X} = 6.80$	$\overline{X} = 7.00$	$\overline{X} = 7.00$	$\overline{X} = 9.40$	$\overline{X} = 7.40$
$S_x = 1.92$	$S_x = 2.24$	$S_x = 2.83$	$S_x = 0.89$	$S_x = 1.14$

Grand Mean: 7.48

Standard Error of the mean: 0.98

Population Mean: 7.60

Population Standard Deviation: 1.96   N = 40

Inferential Concepts

A major interest of a researcher, or an individual involved in performing an evaluation, might be to explore a population of analysis units by some sampling procedure to gain a keener insight into the behavior of the characteristics of interest. In addition, researchers may be interested in confirming some belief, or hypothesis, relative to characteristics within the population. In either situation, a sample, or samples, is to be selected from the population of interest and some statement made, based upon the sample data, about the population characteristic(s). For example, an analyst may believe that the more crowded a classroom (in terms of space and/or numbers of students) the more likely it will be that student achievement levels decline, all other influencing factors being held constant. Clearly, the researcher will need to select a sample or samples and, based upon the sample results, make some generalization or inference to the population(s) from which the sample(s) was selected. This process is referred to as **statistical inference** (*) and is the subject addressed in the balance of this chapter.

Estimation versus Hypothesis Testing

Let's consider two aspects of statistical inference [Hereafter, we'll call this **inference** (*).]. The first of these, referred to as **estimation** (*), occurs when one is using sample data to gain information (usually unknown) about a population of interest, generally estimating some parameter such as the arithmetic mean. Associated with estimates, based upon sample data, will be errors that are not controllable by the researcher, namely, sampling errors. The researcher who believes that data are sufficiently important to merit reporting is obligated to inform the users of the possible errors, especially if the researcher has reason to believe that the data are subject to large errors. But, even if the possible errors are relatively small, the researcher should report this fact. Should this not be done, the reader of an article or paper using sample data will be unable to use the data with the amount of confidence the data deserves. (Even newspaper articles reporting the results of surveys are beginning to report the precision and associated confidence of the estimates from the sample!)

Let's consider the following situation:

> After a teachers' association meeting in a certain large school district, the question arose as to how many persons attended the meeting. One individual estimated 300. Another was more cautious and said around 300; another said between 275 and 325. A fourth person, still more conservative, estimated between 250 and 350. Each estimate increased the possibility of being correct by broadening the range of values that could include the true number. Thus, by increasing the range of possible values, the likelihood (probability) of the estimate being correct is increased. Of course, the range can be increased so much that the estimate becomes useless.

The second aspect of inference to be discussed in this chapter is referred to as **hypothesis testing** (*). Just what is an hypothesis? It is a belief or statement that may be made in order to test the validity of some situation. It may be termed a tentative assumption about the world around us. It may be based upon prior research findings conducted in a related subject area. In educational research, an example of a **research hypothesis** (*) might be that "reduction in class size has a positive effect on student achievement." To test this hypothesis would require collecting data under controlled conditions by establishing an appropriate experimental or quasi–experimental design. (This Manual will not dwell on the subject of designing experiments. The reader is referred to several of the references on experimental design.) Another research hypothesis that might require some type of experimental design would be that "teachers become more effective with training and experience."

Still another hypothesis might be that "younger teachers have different opinions from teachers with longer tenure on a number of issues affecting the teaching profession." This research hypothesis could be assessed by designing a survey sampling plan and would require identifying the population of teachers of interest and then following through with the development of a survey instrument and the actual sampling of teachers. (This Manual will not dwell on the subject of **survey sampling** (*). The reader is referred to several of the references on this topic.)

Research Hypotheses, Research Questions, and Statistical Hypotheses.

It should be noted that research hypotheses could also be expressed as **research questions** (*). Consider the previously mentioned three research hypotheses and possible associated research questions:

    1. **Research hypothesis**: "Reduction in class size has a positive effect on student achievement."

     Research question: "Does the reduction in class size have a positive effect on student achievement?"

    2. **Research hypothesis**: "Teachers become more effective with training and experience."

     Research question: "Do teachers become more effective with training and experience?"

    3. **Research hypothesis**: "Younger teachers have different opinions from teachers with longer tenure on a number of issues affecting the teaching profession."

     Research question: "Do younger teachers have different opinions from teachers with longer tenure on a number of issues affecting the teaching profession?"

Generally speaking, a research hypothesis will be based upon prior research or studies, while a research question may be associated with a problem, dilemma or issue on which little or no prior research or studies have been conducted.

In addition to understanding the research hypothesis and research question, it is important before diving into actual inferential techniques that the reader understand a third related concept, that of **statistical hypotheses** (*) and **null hypotheses** (*). In theory, once a research hypothesis or research question has been established, the researcher will begin to collect the data that will lead to the rejection or acceptance (hereafter more appropriately referred to as non–rejection) of the hypothesis or question. In practice, however, many research hypotheses or questions do not lend themselves to hypotheses which can be easily tested. To illustrate, consider the following two examples which relate to two of the research hypotheses raised above:

    "Reduction in class size has a positive effect on student achievement."

To test such an hypothesis requires setting bounds on the statement. Some of the issues to be resolved before any testing can occur are: How will achievement be measured? What class size ranges will be included? What grade levels in school will be considered? What about the impact of teaching methods and individual teachers? What is meant by "has a positive effect on achievement?" To test the hypothesis as it is now worded requires answering all of the above questions and possibly more. Let's consider just one of the questions. Since the phrase "has a positive effect on achievement" may mean different things to different researchers, it may be more appropriate to reword the hypothesis as follows: "Reduction in class size has no effect on achievement of students." This new hypothesis, which most of us would understand, is referred to as the "statistical hypothesis" and, in this case, as the "null hypothesis" (i.e., no effect exists).

    "Younger teachers have different opinions from teachers with longer tenure on a number of issues affecting the teaching profession."

This statement is somewhat broad and needs to be qualified before data collection occurs. Some of the questions which must be answered before an appropriate sampling plan can be developed are: What are the issues of importance? How are "younger" teachers defined? By age? By years of teaching experience? What is meant by "longer tenure?" What part of the teaching profession is of interest? Specifically, what is meant by "have different opinions?" This phrase could be interpreted differently by different researchers: to be different, opinions must differ by 5%? by 10%? by 25%? To avoid this situation, the above hypothesis might be reworded as follows: "Younger teachers do not have different opinions from teachers with longer tenure on a number of issues affecting the teaching profession." Once again, a statistical (and also a null) hypothesis has been developed. Most of us could agree on what is meant by "no difference."

An examination of the above two situations should point to a common observation–the researcher is stating that there is no difference or no effect:

1. "Reduction in class size has no effect ...."

2. "Younger teachers do not have different opinions..."

The research hypothesis and/or question has been converted into an hypothesis that effectively states that whatever it is that is being studied has no effect or impact. In other words, a null hypothesis.

Risk, Confidence, and Types of Errors

By establishing the statistical hypothesis, the researcher is indicating that the hypothesis will be rejected if large enough differences are observed in the sample(s) that the likelihood that the null hypothesis is true is very small. Imagine, if you will, tossing a coin 100 times. If you observed 55 heads and 45 tails you might be willing to attribute this departure from 50:50 due to chance alone. However, if your results showed 80 heads and 20 tails, you'd probably say that something happened beyond what you might expect to observe due to chance alone. Perhaps the one tossing the coin was an expert in forcing the results to turn up heads more than tails. Or, perhaps the coin was weighted towards heads and was, therefore, a biased coin. Regardless of which of these two (and possibly other) situations existed, you would probably be willing to conclude that chance alone could not have caused such a great difference from your null hypothesis of 50:50.

Hypothesis testing, therefore, involves **tests of significance** (*) in which the difference between two or more measures is compared to determine whether this difference might have occurred by chance alone (recall our discussion on sampling distributions earlier in this chapter) in simple random sampling. If the observed difference(s) is larger (by some criteria) than one might expect by chance alone when sampling under the assumption that the null hypothesis is true, the hypothesis is rejected. And, the results are said to be statistically significant with some risk that the rejection is not correct. These risks, in educational research, are most frequently 0.10, 0.05, or 0.01.

Consider the risk of 0.10. In selecting this risk in advance of conducting our research we are really stating: If under the hypothesis(es) being tested the probability of observing the differences in my set of data is 0.10 or less, then I will reject my null hypothesis and conclude that the observed differences exceed what I would expect by chance alone in random sampling from the population(s) under study. This risk is referred to as the **level of significance** (*) or **risk** (*), associated with hypothesis testing. The selection of the particular risk associated with a false rejection of an hypothesis is really not a statistical issue but rather a practical issue. One might ask the question: If I reject the null hypothesis falsely and take some course of action, what is the risk associated with my taking such a wrong action? If the risk is great (e.g., committing large sums of money), then one would want the statistical risk to be very small, say 0.01 or even less.

Now, if we do reject a null hypothesis at a pre–determined risk level, say 0.05, then we can also state that in rejecting the null hypothesis we are doing so with 95% confidence or better. This is referred to in statistical jargon as the **level of confidence** (*). It should be clear that a low risk (level of significance) has associated with it a high level of confidence. The Greek letter alpha–α–is used to denote the level of significance, or risk. Conversely, $1-\alpha$, is used to identify the associated level of confidence.

To illustrate the concepts of risk and confidence, let's consider the example above on teacher opinions. Suppose all necessary issues bearing on the study have been resolved and a sample of 200 teachers from each of two tenure categories has been randomly selected from the population of interest. Responses for these 400 on one of the issues shows a disagreement of 0.05 (e.g., the younger teachers favor the issue by 0.55 and the other teachers by 0.60). Is this difference of 0.05 large enough to conclude that there is a difference on this issue within the population from which the samples were selected? What if the difference were 0.10? 0.02? It should be evident that the larger the difference the more likely that the hypothesis of no difference in opinions is wrong. But how large does this difference have to be?

The larger the sample size the greater the ability to detect smaller differences as being statistically significant. But, what constitutes statistical significance? What confidence does the researcher want in order to reject the null hypothesis? Certainly the greater the confidence in rejecting the lower the risk. So, it is essential that the researcher specify the risk or confidence needed to reject the null hypothesis. As stated earlier, the selection of risk or confidence is not a statistical issue but rather a practical issue, one which depends on the impact of making a wrong decision, such as rejecting a null hypothesis when it should not have been rejected.

Since risks are inherent in any sampling process, it is important to recognize that the researcher could be committing one of two types of errors. The first of these would occur when rejecting the null hypothesis when it should not be rejected. This is referred to as a **Type I error** (*) and its likelihood is determined by the risk level, or alpha.

On the other hand, it is possible that one might not reject the null hypothesis when it should have been rejected. Such a situation is referred to as committing a **Type II error** (*), not rejecting the null hypothesis when it should have been rejected. In this Manual we dwell on the Type I error and **remind the reader frequently to keep in mind that a non–rejection still has some possible errors associated with it**. In other words, a non–rejection of the null hypothesis does not mean it is necessarily true. In fact, from a practical perspective parameters of interest, such as averages or percentages, are probably not the same in any two populations under study. The main issue is whether the differences are large enough for the analyst to be willing to recommend a rejection of a null hypothesis with the actions which would follow from such a rejection.

Now, let's consider several estimation situations and then a larger number of examples which call for hypothesis testing.

Estimation

In the previous section a distinction was made between problems associated with estimation and those related to hypothesis testing. This section examines two specific situations in which the estimation aspect of statistical inference is applied. Basically, in estimation we are selecting a sample from a population and using information in the sample to provide an estimate of a population parameter. While the concept carries over to other parameters, this section reviews the approach in estimating proportions or percentages and averages. Now, let's recall how the concepts of risk and confidence enter into the estimation process. Any sample statistic can be used to estimate the corresponding population parameter. The statistic, since it is based upon sample information only, is subject to variability. As we saw earlier in this chapter, the same sample statistic from a series of random samples drawn from the same population will differ from sample to sample. And, all other things being held under control, these differences in the sample statistics can be attributed to chance variation only. So, what is needed is a process to describe the amount of **error** (*) or **precision** (*) in our estimate of the population parameter as well as the confidence we desire to associate with this lack of precision. Let's recall formula 7.2 and see how it may well be an approach to helping us arrive at a measure of precision and confidence. Formula 7.2 is repeated here:

$$X = \mu \pm Z * \sigma$$

where μ and σ are the mean and standard deviation of the population respectively. Recall also that the symbol * means to multiply. By appropriate selection of the value for Z we can identify ranges about the arithmetic mean which contain a specified percentage of the population values. Isn't it possible for us to do the same thing using our standard error of the mean in place of the standard deviation of the population? Certainly. So, formula 7.2 now becomes:

$$X = \mu \pm Z * \sigma_{\bar{X}} \tag{7.4}$$

With the population mean and standard deviation known, it would be possible to establish a range about the population mean which would contain a certain percentage of the sample means drawn randomly from that population. If we assume we are looking at Z = 1.96, then we would be including 95% of the sample means within this range. We refer to the±1.96 (plus and minus) limits as being the 95% limits for the sample means drawn from the same population. In a similar way it is possible to construct limits about a single sample mean, using only information in a sample, such that there is 95% confidence that the limits contain the population mean. Such limits are referred to as 95% **confidence limits** (*). A more detailed discussion of the formulas associated with the process of developing confidence limits can be found in Mohr (1990).

Proportions (Percentages)

Let's consider our database titled 2SCH4. Recall that this database consists of records for 224 graduates at a given high school over a three year period. In creating the database, initially the sex of the individual AU appears in Appendix E, Column 3, with a 1 indicating a male and a 2 indicating a female. This same attribute has been recoded (See column 14) so that a male is identified by a 0 and a female by a 1. If we were to add up the 0's and 1's and then divided by 224, the number of students in the sample, we would have an indicator of the proportion of females in the population. In fact, there were 107 females and 117 males. Therefore, the proportion of females can be seen to be 107/224 = 0.478.

Although SEX is an attribute, since it is binomial, we can make use of the descriptive statistics report to compute the average of the 0's and 1's. This average is, effectively, equivalent to the proportion of 1's in the sample. Now, let's look at the Descriptive Statistics module of our statistical software and calculate (or rather let our software calculate) the average for this binomial attribute. Exhibit 7.7, which follows, is a reduced reproduction of the Descriptive Statistics printout for the attribute SEX, found in Appendix E.

EXHIBIT 7.7 DESCRIPTIVE STATISTICS FOR THE ATTRIBUTE SEX FROM THE
2SCH4 DATABASE

Mean–Average	*.4776786*	No. observations	224
Lower 95% c.i.limit	*.4121195*	No. missing values	0
Upper 95% c.i.limit	*.5432376*	Sum of frequencies	224

The average, as reported in the second row of Exhibit 7.7 is seen to be .478, or 47.8%. This means that 47.8% of the sample can be identified as females. The next two rows, immediately under the "Mean–Average," identify the 95% confidence limits for the population proportion (Please see *bold/italicized* items in Exhibit 7.7), assuming that this is a random sample drawn from a population. These limits are seen to be:

Lower 95% limit:.412

Upper 95% limit:.543

These limits can be interpreted in the following way: based upon the sampling process employed, there is a 95% probability (chance) that the population proportion lies somewhere between .412 and .543. The converse of this is also true, namely, there is a 5% chance that the true population proportion lies outside of these limits. We can also note that the distance between the sample proportion and each of the two limits (allowing for rounding) is .065. We might also state that the population proportion lies somewhere in the range:

.478±.065

As stated earlier in this section, the number±.065 is referred to as the error in the estimate or the precision of the estimate.

One should note that if a different random sample were taken from the same population, the estimate would undoubtedly differ from the .478 and the precision would also differ slightly. These differences, assuming we sample randomly, can be attributed to chance alone.

One final observation, although we usually will never know whether our confidence limits actually include the population parameter being estimated, we can be assured that the methodology employed will give us 90%, 95% or 99% confidence that the actual parameter (proportion or average) has been located.

Averages

Now, once again using our 2SCH4 database, let's assume that our sample of 224 has been drawn from a known population and that we wish to estimate the average grade point average in the population based upon the sample average. The Descriptive Statistics panel from Appendix E for the grade point average variable is partially reproduced as Exhibit 7.8. It can be seen from this exhibit that the average grade point average is 2.967. Below this average in Exhibit 7.8 are seen the upper and lower 95% confidence limits. (Please see *bold/italicized* items in Exhibit 7.8.) These limits are:

Lower confidence limit: 2.902

Upper confidence limit: 3.032

EXHIBIT 7.8 DESCRIPTIVE STATISTICS FOR THE
VARIABLE GRADE POINT AVERAGE FROM THE 2SCH4 DATABASE

Mean - Average	*2.966786*	No. observations	224
Lower 95% c.i.limit	*2.901575*	No. missing values	0
Upper 95% c.i.limit	*3.031997*	Sum of frequencies	224

One can, therefore, state that the 95% confidence limits range from 2.902 to 3.032. The error or precision is seen as±.066 (except for rounding discrepancies). (**Please note: the fact that the error associated with the proportion example in the previous section is the same as for this illustration is a coincidence!!**)

We can now state that we have used a method which gives us 95% confidence that the true population average for the variable grade point average lies somewhere between 2.902 and 3.032. Recall again, that another sample drawn from the same population would probably yield a different average and a slightly different precision. Note that if 90% confidence limits were desired the range would be smaller, more precision but less confidence, while if 99% confidence limits were desired, the range would be greater, indicating less precision, but more confidence.

Now, let's consider a second example of confidence limits for an average. For the same database, 2SCH4, let's look at the SAT Verbal scores (Column 6 of the database). Appearing in Exhibit 7.9 is part of the Descriptive Statistics panel for the SAT Verbal variable, taken from Appendix D. From this panel the average verbal SAT score for the 224 students is seen to be 426.5. The lower and upper 95% confidence limits (Please see ***bold/italicized*** items in Exhibit 7.9.) are seen to be:

Lower 95% confidence limit: 413.3

Upper 95% confidence limit: 439.8

EXHIBIT 7.9 DESCRIPTIVE STATISTICS FOR THE
VARIABLE VERBAL SAT SCORES FROM THE 2SCH4 DATABASE

Mean–Average	*426.5179*	No. observations	224
Lower 95% c.i.limit	*413.272*	No. missing values	0
Upper 95% c.i.limit	*439.7637*	Sum of frequencies	224

Except for a rounding difference, the precision or error is seen to be±13.3 units (439.8–426.5). Our interpretation for these limits is that there is a 95% chance that the method employed in estimating the average verbal SAT score in the population from which this sample was drawn has located the true average SAT Verbal score as lying somewhere between 413.3 and 439.8. Recall again that there is no guarantee that the population average has been located, only that there is a 95% chance that it has been located.

Hypothesis Testing

In the previous section the inferential concept of estimation was introduced. In this section attention is directed towards the concept of hypothesis testing. An earlier section compares these two inferential approaches. The reader is reminded that in hypothesis testing there needs to be an hypothesis to test. Hypothesis testing generally results from either the specification of a research question or a research hypothesis.

In this manual the following inferential situations are addressed from the hypothesis testing perspective:

Testing Contingency Tables: 2x2 and rxc

Testing Averages: Two; More Than Two; Linear Comparisons; Two–Way; and Analysis of covariance

Testing Two or More Than Two Characteristics: Correlation and Regression; and Discriminant Analysis

Selected Non–Parametric Procedures

First, however, let's review the basic concepts of testing statistical hypotheses. Consider a single sample. Assuming that a random sample has been selected from a well–defined population, a sample statistic, such as a proportion (e.g., the proportion who favor an issue) or an average (e.g., the mean income) has been computed. The hypothesis being tested might be that the sample was drawn from a population with a specified proportion or a specified average value. The process then involves selecting a risk, or level of significance, such as .05 or .01. The sample statistic is then compared with the population parameter to determine whether the observed difference (and there will usually be one) could be attributed to chance alone, or whether this difference is sufficiently large that it is highly unlikely (confidences of 95% or 99% associated with the specified risks) that the sample could have been drawn from the population with the specified parameter. This comparison is accomplished through observing a p **value** (*) (or, sometimes referred to as a "prob" or **"probability" value** (*)). If this p value is small, namely, less than the selected level of significance (recall that this level of significance or risk is represented by the Greek letter alpha, α), then the likelihood or probability that the observed differences could have been due to chance alone in random sampling is sufficiently small so that we are willing to reject the null hypothesis and conclude that the observed differences are in fact real.

An Algorithm for Hypothesis Testing

Now, having said all this, let's establish an algorithm which should be extremely useful in doing our hypothesis testing:

1.   Some issue, problem, or situation has generated a research question or a   research hypothesis.

2.   The research question or research hypothesis is then converted into a null or statistical hypothesis.

3.   A level of significance, or risk, is then selected, based upon similar studies in the past or considerations of the implications due to making wrong decisions as a consequence of sampling. The level of significance is usually represented by the Greek letter alpha, α .

4.   The appropriate analysis method is next selected based upon the specific hypothesis, or hypotheses, being tested.

5.   Upon completion of the appropriate analysis (or the massaging of the data by your personal computer) it is next necessary to locate the "p" value or "prob" value. This value represents the proba-

bility of observing the given sample results (or results more extreme) if the statistical hypothesis were true.

6.   Two conclusions are possible:

    6.1 If the observed "p" value is less than the alpha value, then the statistical hypothesis is rejected and you can conclude with a specified confidence (depending upon the α level selected) that your statistical hypothesis is false.

    6.2 If the observed "p" value is greater than or equal to the alpha value, then the statistical hypothesis may not be rejected and you would conclude that the sample results are not inconsistent with the statistical hypothesis, at the level of significance which you have selected. NOTE: your conclusion is not that you accept the statistical hypothesis. A non–rejection does not imply acceptance of the statistical hypothesis, as there are many other possible hypotheses which could just as well have not been rejected at your level of significance.

In the sections which follow, several hypothesis testing methodologies will be presented. The approach will be to carry through a single example of each hypothesis testing situation, developing the rationale for each successive step. Then one or more additional examples will be introduced but the methodology will not change. In each instance, the issue which has created a need for sampling and the collection of data is described. Next, the final conclusion for the specific example is presented.

Contingency Tables: 2x2 and rxc.

Three examples follow. The first is a detailed illustration of the process of testing an hypothesis when the data are to be presented in a 2x2 contingency table (i.e., two columns and two rows of data). As discussed in Chapter 5 (A good review of Chapter 5 might be appropriate now.), such tables are often referred to as **cross–tabulations** (*) or just simply **cross–tabs** (*). They actually are frequency or percentage distributions, depending upon how the data are described. The second example is also for a 2x2 contingency table but without the detailed calculations. The third example has two columns and five rows. This is referred to as a 2x5 or a 5x2 contingency table. In general contingency tables greater than a 2x2 are referred to as rxc tables (number of rowsxnumber of columns). In this manual we only consider the 2x2 and a 2x5. There are also three–way contingency tables which permit one to test hypotheses when the data are classified in three ways rather than two. To illustrate, a survey might be conducted to examine differences in opinions on specific issues (1) based upon SEX (2) and POLITICAL PARTY (3). This would call for utilizing a three–way contingency table and an analysis referred to as log–linear analysis.

Example A: Consider a survey which has been conducted based upon a random sample of 500 individuals from a large population. Assume further that all 500 of those in the sample responded to the survey, a situation which is clearly unrealistic. This assumption is made here so that adjustments for non–response (somewhat complex adjustments in some cases) do not have to be considered. Several demographics, such as age, sex, and marital status, have been asked of the respondents. In addition numerous opinion items were included, several of which called for a simple YES or NO response. Exhibit 7.10 is a table which indicates how males and females responded to one of the YES or NO items. This exhibit includes not only the responses of the males and females to a single opinion item, but it also includes additional numerical values. The intent of these values, the subsequent computations, and the discussion which follow is to familiarize the reader with the concept of "testing a null hypothesis."

Let's first review the meaning of the entries in the body of the table. (Please see Chapter 5 for additional examples.) The intersection of a column, say MALE, and a row, say YES, is referred to as a **cell** (*). The cell which represents the MALE and YES intersections has within it three values:

60   This represents the number of MALES in the sample who responded YES to this specific item.

(30%)   This represents the percentage of MALES who responded YES out of the 200 MALES (See the last row labeled TOTALS) who were in the final sample.

(78)   This represents the expected number of MALES who should have responded YES if the null hypothesis (to be stated in a moment) were in fact true. (We'll find how we can obtain this number shortly.)

EXHIBIT 7.10 MALE AND FEMALE RESPONSES TO AN OPINION ITEM ON A SAMPLE SURVEY: A 2x2 CONTINGENCY TABLE1

		SEX		
		MALE	FEMALE	TOTALS
RESPONSE				
YES		60 (30%)	135 (45%)	195 (39%)
		(78)	**(117)**	
NO		140 (70%)	165 (55%)	305 (61%)
		(122)	**(183)**	
TOTALS	200	300		500

1–Bold items in ( ) represent expected frequencies under the assumption that the null hypothesis is true.

As a second example, consider the cell which represents the intersection of the column labeled FEMALE and the row labeled NO:

165   This represents the number of FEMALES in the sample who responded NO to this specific item.

(55%)   This represents the percentage of FEMALES who responded NO out of the 300 FEMALES (See the last row labeled TOTALS) who were in the final sample.

(183)   This represents the expected number of FEMALES who should have responded NO if the null hypothesis (to be stated in a moment) were in fact true.

The last column labeled TOTALS gives the total number of YES and NO responses, independent of whether the respondent was a MALE or a FEMALE. The numbers in ( ) represent the percentage of YES and NO responses in this sample.

Now, let's consider what issue might be addressed by using these data. Suppose this survey was being conducted to determine whether there were any differences in opinions among the respondents when considering specific demographics. The intent might be to determine whether it would be necessary to differentiate between specific demographic groups, say MALES and FEMALES, in developing a political campaign. If differences were found to exist in the sample (and assuming we have randomly sampled and have a high response rate), then a decision would need to be made with respect to the direction of the campaign. On the other hand, if no statistical differences were detected, then the campaign might be geared towards the voters, independent of their sex. Now what might be an appropriate null hypothesis to test? Actually, several come to mind:

1.   The response to this specific item on the survey is independent of the SEX of the person.

2.   There is no relationship between the response to this item and the SEX of the person.

3.   The distribution of responses to this item is not related to the SEX of the individual.

These are actually three different ways of stating the same null hypothesis. Note that we are dealing with percentages, proportions, or frequencies in this analysis.

Now, let's work our way through the process for arriving at the expected frequencies under the assumption that the null hypothesis is true (Don't panic; this will be the only time we'll plow our way through these calculations on how the expected frequencies are developed).

1. Under the assumption that the null hypothesis is true (i.e., there is no difference in the response patterns for males and females), what would be the   best estimate of the proportion of AUs in the population who would be expected to say YES? Right, it's got to be 195/500 = .39 (or 39%). Of those who responded, independent of their SEX , 195 or 39% said YES.

2. Now, assuming that the 39% is our best estimate of the percentage saying YES in the population, how many of the 200 MALES would be expected to have said YES? Right, again, 39% of the 200 or 78, the number which appears in ($\overline{X}$) below the 60 MALES who responded YES in the sample.

3. Since the number of responding MALES must add up to 200, it should be clear that the expected number of MALES saying NO should be 122 (200–78).

4. Since 195 said YES in the sample and since 78 were expected to be MALES, it must follow that 117 would be expected to be FEMALES saying YES (195–78 = 117).

5. Finally, since the number of responding females must add up to 305, the number of FEMALES responding NO should be 165 (305–122 = 183).

Let's ask ourselves how we might logically measure whether the differences between the four observed cell frequencies and the four expected cell frequencies (assuming the null hypothesis were true) represent an acceptable chance variation or whether the probability of these differences existing by chance alone is small (say less than an α of .05). For the cell in which 60 MALES responded YES there were 78 expected frequencies under the null hypothesis. We were off by –18 (60–78). If we look at the same differences for the other four cells, we see the following differences:

MALES/YES:	60 – 78 = – 18
MALES/NO:	140 – 122 = + 18
FEMALES/YES:	135 – 117 = + 18
FEMALES/NO:	165 – 183 = – 18

Clearly the differences add to 0:–18,+18,+18, and –18. This will always be the case when comparing the observed to the expected frequencies. To eliminate this summing to 0 the differences are squared and then divided by the expected cell frequencies as noted below:

$$(60–78)^2/78 \quad = (–18)^2/78 \quad = 4.15$$

$$(140–122)^2/122 = (+18)^2/122 = 2.66$$

$$(135–117)^2/117 = (+18)^2/117 = 2.77$$

$$(165–183)^2/183 = (–18)^2/183 = 1.77$$

The sum of these four numbers is seen to be 11.35 and is referred to as chi–square (The symbol for chi–square is χ^2, a symbol which we shall not use further in this manual.) Now, the question which arises is whether this value (11.35) is sufficiently large that we must conclude the null hypothesis is highly unlikely and, hence, we would reject the null hypothesis. Classically, in hypothesis testing one would utilize a chi–square table (with appropriate degrees of freedom, which are related to the number of cells in the contingency table) at the risk or level of significance for the analysis. This table would indicate a value of chi–square such that a calculated chi–square greater than the tabular value would result in a rejection of the null hypothesis. Fortunately, we are able to avoid the use of such tables. The software used in this manual, as well as most other available statistical software, takes the calculated value for chi–square and converts it to a "p" or probability that the observed differences, or greater, could have occurred by chance alone if the null hypothesis were true. A small "p" suggests that the null hypothesis is probably false and, hence, may be rejected. (**HINT: review the Algorithm for Hypothesis Testing** presented earlier in this chapter.) This capability of these statistical software packages eliminates the need for using look–up tables and also, in the opinion of the author of this manual, gives a more understandable number for purposes of analyzing the sample results.

For this example, the "p" value associated with the calculated chi–square would be given as p = 001. If the level of significance (recall, this is α) were taken at .05, or even .01, then since the "p" value is less than the α value, the null hypothesis would be rejected with better than 99% confidence.

We are not through yet, however. Once the statistical conclusion has been drawn, it is essential to relate this to the issue or problem which generated the need for the survey. An examination of these data shows that 30% of the MALES and 45% of the FEMALES would vote YES for this issue. One is forced to conclude that a greater percentage of FEMALES would support the issue. Now, it's time to determine what this means from an operational point of view. Do we develop a campaign to address MALES and FEMALES

differently, or do we mount a campaign to convince both males and females that this is an issue on which they should both be convinced to vote YES. From here on the actions become non–statistical in nature.

Example B: In a given school district it was of interest to assess possible relationships among various demographics. Among the demographics which were being considered were SEX of the student and NUMBER OF YEARS EXPERIENCE WITH A PERSONAL COMPUTER (let's shorten this to YEARS). The null hypothesis would be that YEARS OF EXPERIENCE with a personal computer was independent of whether the individual was a MALE or a FEMALE. Assume that $\alpha = .05$ and the results of the survey are as in Exhibit 7.11.

The chi–square test for this cross–tabulation of SEX by YEARS was found to yield a p value of .5789. Now, using this p value we conclude that we have insufficient grounds to reject the null hypothesis. Why did this occur? If we examine the data in Exhibit 7.11 we see that of those with 0–1 years of experience 63% were MALES and 37% were FEMALES. Of those with 2–4 years of experience, 67% were MALES and 33% were FEMALES. Of those with 5 or more years of experience 52% were MALES and 48% were FEMALES. The results of our analysis suggest that even though there is a difference in the proportion of MALES and FEMALES in each of the three categories it is not sufficiently great for us to be willing to reject the null hypothesis at the level of significance selected.

EXHIBIT 7.11 MALE AND FEMALE YEARS OF EXPERIENCE IN THE
USE OF A PERSONAL COMPUTER1

SEX	Years of Experience			Total
	0–1	2–4	5 or more	
MALE	19 (63%)	8 (67%)	14 (52%)	41 (59%)
	(18)	**(7)**	**(16)**	
FEMALE	11 (37%)	64 (33%)	13 (48%)	28 (41%)
	(12)	**(5)**	**(11)**	
Total	30	12	27	69

p = .5789;1) bold numbers in ( ) represent expected frequencies assuming the null hypothesis is true. NOTE: Percentages in ( ) read down each column in the exhibit.

Example C: Let's assume that a survey has been conducted with a sample of 247 being obtained randomly from this same population. Assume further that it is of interest to determine whether there are any differences between MALES and FEMALES in assessing the relative importance of various issues. The results of the survey for a single issue appear in Exhibit 7.12 where the "importance" scale was given as extremely unimportant, unimportant, uncertain, important, extremely important. This scale is referred to as a **Likert scale** (*) and is used quite often in opinion and attitudinal surveys.

EXHIBIT 7.12 A COMPARISON OF MALE AND FEMALE RESPONSES
TO A FIVE ITEM LIKERT QUESTION ON A SURVEY1

| | SEX | | |
| **RESPONSE** | | | |
CATEGORY	**MALE**	**FEMALE**	**TOTAL**
Extremely	7 (4.5%)	2 (2.2%)	9 (3.6%)
Unimportant	**(6)**	**(3)**	**(9)**
Unimportant	49 (31.4%)	15 (16.5%)	64 (25.9%)
	(40)	**(24)**	**(64)**
Uncertain	33 (21.2%)	18 (19.8%)	51 (20.6%)
	(32)	**(19)**	**(51)**
Important	42 (26.9%)	40 (44.0%)	82 (33.2%)
	(52)	**(30)**	**(82)**
Extremely	25 (16.0%)	16 (17.6%)	41 (16.6%)
Important	**(26)**	**(15)**	**(41)**
Total	156	91	247

p = 0.0274;1) bold numbers in ( ) represent expected frequencies assuming the null hypothesis is true. NOTE: once again, the percentages in ( ) read down each column.

The null hypothesis would be that the distribution of attitudes did not differ between MALES and FEMALES. Assume a level of significance of .05. The results of the analysis yielded a p value of .0274, which clearly indicates a rejection of the null hypothesis. For such a rejection to occur it would require that the distributions of the "importance" scales were sufficiently different between males and females that the probability of chance causing the difference would be extremely small. In this case, the p value of .0274 calls for a rejection of the null hypothesis with better than 95% confidence (Note that, had $\alpha = .01$, the null hypothesis would not have been rejected. This means that rejection can occur with better than 95% confidence but not 99% confidence.)

Now, what has lead to this rejection? Looking at the data in Exhibit 7.12, since we can conclude that the distributions of "importance" responses are significantly different, where does it appear that the real differences lie? As we examine Exhibit 7.12, the first real difference shows up in the "Unimportant" category with 31.4% of the males and 16.5% of the females responding to "Unimportant." A second category where the difference becomes obvious is in the "Important" category with 26.9% of the males and 44.0% of the females responding to "Important." Upon further examination of Exhibit 7.12 (And, any researcher should know his or her data intimately), it appears that 35.9% of the males and only 18.7% of the females consider the issue as either "extremely unimportant" or "unimportant." On the other hand, 42.9% of the males and 61.6% of the females consider the issue as either "important" or "extremely important." [Note: this process of combining adjacent cells is frequently referred to as collapsing (*).] What would you conclude from this analysis? Of course, on a relative basis this issue is more important to the females than to the males.

Unfortunately, conclusions which occur with rejections of null hypotheses are not always as obvious as for this set of data. However, a clear understanding of the data will usually lead the researcher to presenting more than just a statistical statement of rejection or non–rejection. Remember, statistics is a tool to provide information which can be useful in making research, evaluation, and management decisions. Using visuals, such as bar charts, can enhance a discussion of the findings (See discussion in Chapter 4.).

Now, let's move on to our discussion of hypothesis testing when we consider averages or arithmetic means, as opposed to frequency distributions or percentages.

Averages: Two; More Than Two; Linear Comparisons; Two–Way; Analysis of Covariance

Very frequently in research or evaluation studies it is of interest to determine whether observed differences (and they will usually be there) between two or more averages can be attributed to chance (random sampling variability) or whether the observed differences exceed what one might expect in random sampling from a single population. This concept, a continuation of what we have already discussed earlier in this chapter on hypothesis testing, is the essence of what we will be considering in the balance of this section. This section considers analysis of two samples, more than two samples, a topic referred to as "**linear comparisons (*)**," a two–way analysis of mean differences, [These analyses are frequently referred to under the name **ANOVA (*)**] and an analysis of means when considering the possible effect of one or more independent variables [usually referred to as the **analysis of covariance** (*) or **ANCOVA (*)**].

Two Sample Averages

Let's assume that we wish to test the null hypothesis that two samples were drawn from a population (or populations) having the same arithmetic mean or average. Recall that the database labeled 2SCH4 (See Appendix E) consists of a sample of 224 students. Assume further that these students represent a random sample from all students within this school district. Our interest is whether there is a significant difference in the average SAT–VERBAL Score between male and female students within the population from which this sample was drawn. We refer to the characteristic SEX as a single **factor** (*) or as a **main effect** (*).

Now, recall the algorithm which we developed earlier regarding the comparisons to be made between the observed probability or " p " value and the selected level of significance, or risk, referred to as α . Specifically, if the observed p value is equal to or greater than ($\geq$) α , we do not reject the null hypothesis; if the observed p value is less than (<) α, we reject the null hypothesis and conclude that the observed differences exceed what we would expect in random sampling at the given α level.

Suppose the observed SAT–VERBAL Score averages were 433.4 and 419.0 for males and females, respectively. Obviously there is a difference! But, is it large enough for us to conclude that it is significant? The methodology which we will utilize in testing differences among averages is referred to as the **analysis of variance** (*) or simply **ANOVA** (*). Please note that this terminology may seem confusing, since we are really interested in comparing averages and not variances (or standard deviations) in our test of the hypotheses. Actually, the methodology does utilize variances to assess the differences between averages but we really needn't worry ourselves about this subtle distinction.

Now, let us state that the difference between these two averages is not statistically significant since the ANOVA methodology yields us a p value of .2855. As in the chi–square testing, the statistical methodology assesses the observed difference (i.e., the difference between 433.4 and 419.0) to determine the probability that this difference, or greater, could have occurred by chance alone under the assumption that the null hypothesis were true. The ANOVA (regardless of which statistical package is employed) produces a table similar to Exhibit 7.13.

EXHIBIT 7.13 RESULTS OF A COMPARISON BETWEEN
TWO SAMPLE MEANS (2SCH4 DATABASE: Appendix E)

Analysis of Variance Report

ANOVA Table for **Response Variable: SAT–Verbal Score**

Source	DF	Sum–Squares	Mean Square	F–Ratio	Prob
A (SEX)*	1	11664.53	11664.53	1.14	0.2855
ERROR	222	2269820	10224.41		
TOTAL(Adj)	223	2281484			

Data in Column 3 of the 2SCH4 database identify whether the student is a male or a female.

This exhibit, referred to as the Analysis of Variance Report or Table, provides us with an indication of which is the dependent variable, sometimes referred to as the **response** (*) or **outcome** (*) variable. In this example it is seen to be the SAT Verbal Score (Column 6 in the 2SCH4 database). The characteristic by which the AUs (the students) are classified, or categorized, is referred to as the **independent variable** (*) (another statistical misnomer), the factor, or the **classification** (*). In this case, the factor is seen to be SEX which appears in column 3 of our database. Following across the row in which the Factor A is indicated, we see that the Prob column yields a value of 0.2855. Since our α level is being taken as .05, we cannot reject the null hypothesis and must conclude that whatever differences exist between the two SAT Verbal Score averages is not large enough for us to be willing to reject the null hypothesis. Not that we ever would, but if we had selected an α level of .30, what would we conclude regarding the null hypothesis? Right, since the p value of 0.2855 is less than the α of .30, we would reject the null hypothesis. But, what would be our confidence in such a rejection? Right again, only 70% (1–.30). Remember, an α of .05 is really requiring that we have at least 95% confidence before we reject a null hypothesis. While the Analysis of variance is the preferred approach of the author for analyzing mean differences, one will frequently find a "t" test referred to for cases in which there are only two alternatives associated with the desired hypothesis being tested.

Included in Exhibit 7.13 is a column labeled "F–Ratio. In the old days (whatever they were) when we used tables to determine significance of a statistical test, the F–Ratio obtained from the data, and based upon the assumption that the null hypothesis is true, was compared to a table F value and, depending upon whether the calculated F–Ratio was larger or smaller than the table F value, the null hypothesis was rejected or not rejected. Fortunately in today's technological environment, we don't need to use tables such as the F table. They are built into most statistical software and we are able to use the calculated p value and to compare this to the established level of significance (Again refer to the section titled An Algorithm for Hypothesis Testing). So, while F–ratios may appear in computer printouts, we will be using the p values for purposes of examining the null hypothesis.

Now, having said all this (one of my associates' favorite expressions) what steps did we have to take in setting up this study? First of all, we would identify the fact that we needed a random sample from our population of male and female students. Next we would have selected the sample, calculated the arithmetic means, and then exercised the particular statistical package to arrive at the prob or p value which is then compared to the selected risk, or α .

So, we have arrived at a non–rejection when considering a pair of sample means. Let's next consider more than two sample means, a situation in which rejection provides us with an interesting dilemma.

More Than Two Sample Averages:

Now suppose that we find ourselves in the situation where we wish to test an hypothesis regarding a specific dependent (outcome or response) variable in which there are more than two possible groups (levels or categories) associated with the single factor. If we happen to find that a rejection of the null hypothesis is appropriate, we will be confronted with the need to determine where, within the set of more than two sample means, we can conclude that a significant difference exists. This is an important topic and will be discussed in the section immediately following this section. In this section we now examine the process for testing the null hypothesis in which there are more than two sample means involved for a single factor.

Let us assume, for the sake of illustration, that we wish to test the research hypothesis that there is a difference in average SAT–Math scores among graduates at a specific school (represented by the database of 2SCH4 in Appendix E) over a three year period. Assume further that we have selected a random sample of graduates across the three years and find that there are 65, 82, and 77 graduates represented in the three graduating samples.

Now, recall that our null hypothesis becomes: there is no difference in the average SAT–Math score across the three graduating classes. We next must select a level of significance, or risk, for this analysis. Let's assume that our risk will be α = .05. In other words, we are willing to reject the null hypothesis of "no difference in the means within the populations being sampled," provided that the probability of this occurring by chance alone under the null hypothesis is .05 (5%) or less. If we do experience a rejection of the null hypothesis, we can do this with a confidence of 95% (1–0.05 = .95 = 95%) or better. Recall further that our algorithm for hypothesis testing tells us that we will be comparing the observed "p" value (Prob or Probability) with the chosen level of risk (namely, α = .05 in this situation). If $p < \alpha$, we reject the null hypothesis with the desired confidence. We sometimes refer to the factor or classification being examined as a **MAIN EFFECT**. In this analysis, the sample means for the SAT–MATH scores for the three graduating years are:

Year	Average MATH–SAT
1	466.6
2	424.3
3	510.0

We certainly can observe differences among the three sample means; but, are these differences large enough for us to be willing to reject the null hypothesis with the confidence we require. Let's proceed with the data massaging and subsequent analysis.

Exhibit 7.14 is the result of running an analysis on the three samples using the NCSS software package. A table, similar to this, might also be observed using other software

packages. We note that the response variable is seen to be the SAT–MATH score and the single factor (A) is the YEARGRAD (or, year of graduation). From Exhibit 7.14, it is also seen that the resulting "Prob" value is 0.0000. This number can be found by scanning across the row for Factor A and reading the value in the column headed **Prob>F** (Note that this is the designation for the "P" value based upon the sample data.)

EXHIBIT 7.14 RESULTS WHEN A COMPARISON IS MADE AMONG THREE SAMPLE MEANS
(2SCH4 DATABASE: APPENDIX E)

Analysis of Variance Report

ANOVA Table for **Response Variable: SAT–MATH**

Source	DF	Sum–Squares	Mean Square	F–Ratio	Prob>F
A (YEARGRAD)	2	291023.8	145511.9	11.14	**0.0000**
ERROR	221	2886360	13060.45		
TOTAL(Adj)	223	3177384			

Since 0.0000 (which is never true!) is less than the stipulated risk of 0.05, we can reject the null hypothesis and conclude with better than 95% confidence that the null hypothesis can be rejected (Actually, for these results the confidence increases to better than 99.99%.). What does all this statistical jargon mean from the practitioner's perspective? We have sufficient confidence in rejecting the null hypothesis and can conclude, therefore, that the three samples could not have come from populations having the same average SAT–MATH score. But, which of the three years are different from each other?

Since this concept can apply to any analysis in which there are more than two sample means, the next section is devoted to a brief discussion of the methodology available to the analyst.

Linear Comparisons

It should be clear that if a rejection of the null hypothesis occurs when only two sample means are involved, a simple observation of the data will indicate which sample mean is larger (or smaller) than the other. Such is not true when you have more than two sample means. For example, in the situation just examined, Year 2 could be less than Year 1 which could be less than Year 3. But, Year 1 and 2 could be not significantly different from each other, yet both could be different from Year 3. To resolve this dilemma there are a series of methodologies available. Among the most common are Fisher's Least Significant Difference (referred to as the LSD), Duncan's, Newman–Keul's, Tukey's and Scheffe's. These methodologies are referred to as **Linear Comparisons** (*) or **Linear Contrasts** (*). Fortunately, we need not worry about the process for utilizing one of these since our statistical software can provide us with the results of whichever methodology we choose. The various methodologies have certain limitations, which are discussed in numerous texts and articles (See the reference to an article by the author of this Manual.). For our purposes in this Manual, we will use the Fisher's LSD approach to identifying which pairwise differences can be identified as statistically significant. Please note that the Fisher's LSD test to identify which means are different from each other is valid only if the ANOVA process results in the rejection of the null hypothesis.

Now, let's proceed with an analysis of the mean differences. Exhibit 7.15 identifies one way in which an analysis of the mean differences resulting from the ANOVA in Exhibit 7.14 might appear using the Fisher's LSD approach.

EXHIBIT 7.15 A COMPARISON OF MEAN DIFFERENCES USING FISHER'S LSD APPROACH IWHEN A SIGNIFICANT MAIN EFFECT HAS BEEN FOUND IN A ONE–WAY CLASSIFICATION

		Graduation Year		
Graduation Year	*Mean Value*	**2**	**1**	**3**
2	425.2	.	S	S
1	464.2	S	.	S
3	505.1	S	S	.

The mean SAT–MATH values have been arranged in ascending order in the second column of Exhibit 7.15. The Graduation year for each of the mean values appears in column 1 of the exhibit and as headings for the last three columns in the exhibit. Using the letter S the entries in the last three columns of the exhibit identify which pairs of differences are statistically significant at the .05 level. In this situation, all sample means are significantly different from each other.

The reader should notice that the average values reported in Exhibit 7.15 differ slightly from those identified earlier in the discussion about analyzing differences among sample means. These differences are due to calculations associated with the specific software used in this Manual and may or may not appear when other statistical software packages are used.

Two Way

The reader should notice that in the two ANOVA examples just given that possible differences in the averages of a dependent variable were analyzed when considering a single independent characteristic (factor) at a time. In the first illustration, differences in averages for the SAT–VERBAL scores (the dependent variable) were examined when considering whether the subjects were male or female (the single factor). In the second illustration, differences in averages of the SAT–MATH scores (the dependent variable) were examined when considering the year of graduation (the single factor) of the subjects. This analysis of a dependent variable when considering independent characteristics (factors) one at a time (or independently of each other) might not enable the analyst to discover whether the two independent factors acting together might be producing an effect which could not be observed when analyzing the data one factor at a time. Consider now the information in Exhibit 7.16. The data in the body of the table and in the margins represents the average scores for a sample of male and female students (factor A) when considering whether they were being evaluated by a test given in three different subjects (factor B). Assume that the tests were graded and then the actual scores converted to percentiles. The entries in the table represent average percentile scores for male and female students in each of the three subjects. For purposes of this illustration it is assumed that the number of students is the same in each cell of the exhibit.

EXHIBIT 7.16 AVERAGE NORMED PERCENTILE SCORES FOR MALE AND FEMALE STU-DENTS IN THREE DIFFERENT SUBJECTS

SUBJECT	SEX		
	MALE	FEMALE	AVERAGE
A	85	65	75
B	75	75	75
C	65	85	75
Average	**75**	**75**	**75**

If one were to analyze the difference in average percentile scores considering SEX only, the results would indicate no ability to reject the null hypothesis which is: "the average percentile scores among the three subjects for males and females is the same." On the other hand, if one were to ignore SEX and consider only the three different subjects, here too the null hypothesis would not be rejected since there is no difference in average percentile scores among the three subject areas.

Now, it doesn't take too much time spent in looking at the entire exhibit to note that while differences do not exist on average between males and females or among the three subjects, something is going on within the body of the table which is noteworthy. As we move from Subject A to Subject B to Subject C, we note that the average MALE percentiles are decreasing while the average FEMALE percentiles are increasing. This phenomenon in statistical parlance is referred to as an **interaction** (*). An interaction, then, is something which occurs when we consider two factors (or more) at the same time but which cannot be detected when we examine these factors one at a time. Fortunately, in addition to the ANOVA allowing us to address hypotheses about main effects, we can also test hypotheses regarding possible interactions between or among Main Effects. The algorithm which we have used in addressing the Main Effects only also applies to testing hypotheses about interactions.

Now, let's assume that we are still considering a random sample of male and female (Factor A) students drawn from three graduating classes (Factor B). What might our three null hypotheses be? Surely:

Hypothesis A: there is no difference in the average SAT–MATH score between male and female students.

Hypothesis B: there is no difference in the average SAT–MATH score among the three graduating classes.

Hypothesis AB: there is no interaction between the SEX of the student and the Graduating Class with respect to the average SAT–MATH scores.

Exhibit 7.17, which follows, provides a software output where Year of Graduation and SEX are the main effects and the dependent variable is SAT–MATH scores.

EXHIBIT 7.17 RESULTS WHEN A COMPARISON IS MADE BETWEEN MEAN VALUES OF THE SAT–MATH SCORES WHEN THE METHOD USED CLASSIFIES THE DEPENDENT VARIABLE UNDER TWO DIFFERENT FACTORS (A TWO–WAY ANALYSIS OF VARIANCE)

Analysis of Variance Report

ANOVA Table for Response Variable: SAT–MATH

Source	DF	Sum–Squares	Mean Square	F–Ratio	Prob>F
A (**YEARGRAD**)	2	250384.5	125192.3	10.52	**0.0000**
B (**SEX**)	1	269484.8	269484.8	22.65	**0.0000**
AB	2	39666.13	19833.07	1.67	**0.1913**
ERROR	218	2594190	11899.95		
TOTAL(Adj)	223	3177384			

Let's again assume that we are using the .05 level of significance (risk). Considering the information in Exhibit 7.17, the following conclusions may be drawn with respect to the three hypotheses (NOTE: in the discussion which follows the average values are available through the information printed out with this analysis of variance and may be found in different locations in the printouts depending upon the particular software being used.)

Hypothesis A: Since the Prob value of 0.0000 is less than the α value of .05, the null hypothesis may be rejected.

Conclusion A: There is a difference in average SAT–MATH scores between Male and Female students, with the averages being, respectively, 499.8 and 429.8.

Hypothesis B: Since the Prob value of 0.0000 is less than the α value of .05, the null hypothesis may be rejected.

Conclusion B: There is a difference among the three graduating classes with respect to the average SAT–MATH scores. As was true in the case of the one–way analysis of the graduating classes, the same differences would apply (using the Fisher's LSD process). Class 2 has a lower average (425.2) than Class 1 (646.2) and Class 1 has a lower average than does Class 3 (505.1).

Hypothesis AB: Since the Prob value of 0.1913 does exceed the α value of .05, the null hypothesis cannot be rejected.

Conclusion AB: This does not mean that there are no differences in the populations. It only means that if differences exist they are sufficiently small that, based upon these samples, they were not considered statistically significant.

It is now up to the researcher to determine possible reasons why these results have been noted. It is critical to remember that indicating rejection or non–rejection of specific hypotheses is insufficient. These statistical conclusions should be related back to the data and expressed in terms of the dependent variable and the factors. After all, there were undoubtedly reasons for collecting these data and testing hypotheses. Let the interested persons or groups know a little bit more than statistical jargon about your findings.

Consider now another analysis associated with the 2SCH4 data to determine whether there is any relationship between the number of honors level (advanced) math courses taken and the SAT–Math score. Assume further that SEX will remain as the second classification or factor. The analysis of variance for this situation would produce the information found in Exhibit 7.18. It is clear from this exhibit that, since the Prob value associated with the highest level of math courses taken is 0.0000, a null hypothesis of no differences in average SAT–Math scores among those taking different numbers of higher level math courses must be rejected with great confidence. However, with respect to the SEX of the individual, these differences are not statistically different. (NOTE: The reader is cautioned in interpreting data such as presented in this situation. If the numbers of male and female students had been proportional across both the Year of Graduation and the number of honors level courses taken, then the results would have been the same. This lack of proportionality can cause apparent differences to occur when a second and different main effect is used with the same first main effect. Discussions on this issue can be found in the references for the analysis of variance.)

EXHIBIT 7.18 RESULTS WHEN A COMPARISON IS MADE BETWEEN MEAN VALUES OF SAT–MATH SCORES, CONSIDERING THE SEX OF THE INDIVIDUAL AND THE NUMBER OF HONORS LEVEL MATH COURSES TAKEN. (A TWO–WAY ANALYSIS OF VARIANCE)

Analysis of Variance Report

ANOVA Table for Response Variable: SAT–MATH

Source	DF	Sum–Squares	Mean Square	F–Ratio	Prob>F
A (SEX)	1	13070.57	13070.57	2.09	**0.1483**
B (MATHLVL)	5	1213201	242640.2	38.80	**0.0000**
AB	5	16203.87	3240.775	0.52	**0.7623**
ERROR	212	1325788	6253.718		
TOTAL(Adj)	223	3177384			

Analysis of the differences using Fisher's LSD methodology yields the information in Exhibit 7.19 which indicates that the greater the number of honors level math courses a student

takes, on average, the greater will be his or her average SAT-Math score. In addition, with the exception of students taking 0 and 1 honor level courses, which are not significantly different from each other (possibly due to the small sample size for the 0 level students), all other averages are significantly different at $\alpha = .05$.

EXHIBIT 7.19 A COMPARISON OF SAT–MATH AVERAGE SCORES USING FISHER'S LSD METHODOLOGY WHEN CONSIDERING THE NUMBER OF HONORS LEVEL MATH COURSES TAKEN.

No. Honors Math Course (Code)*	Mean SAT–Math	LEVEL CODES* A B C D E F
0 (A)	290.0	. . . S** S S S
1 (B)	358.8	. . S S S S
2 (C)	406.3	S S . S S S
3 (D)	464.4	S S S . S S
4 (E)	557.8	S S S S . S
5 (F)	628.6	S S S S S .

* Represents the assigned code associated with the specific number of honors level math courses taken.

** "S" indicates significant difference between row and column codes; "." indicates no significant difference.

Analysis of Covariance (ANCOVA)

An issue which might be raised is whether or not students taking higher level honors math courses might also be those students with higher GPAs. It is conceivable that the higher GPAs, associated with these honor level students, might have an impact on the evident relationship between increasing numbers of honors level courses and the obvious increase in average SAT–Math scores. After all, don't the brighter students tend to take more honors level courses? Let's examine Exhibit 7.20 which provides a visual comparison between the SAT–Math scores and the GPA Scores for these same students.

The reader is cautioned that there are numerous assumptions associated with using the ANCOVA, the most important of which is that the regressions for the levels of the main effects and the covariates are not different. When this assumption is not met, a bias may be introduced into the final analysis. In addition, it is assumed that the covariate being used has been demonstrated to be reliable, i.e., has little error of measurement.

EXHIBIT 7.20 A COMPARISON OF SAT–MATH SCORES AND GPA SCORES

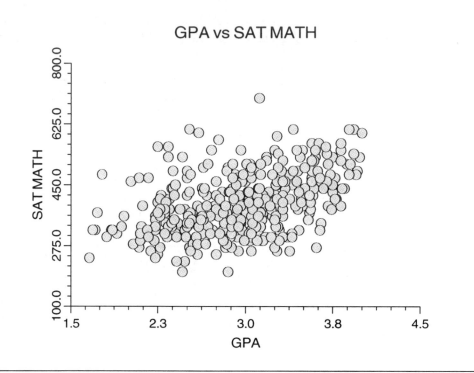

A separate analysis indicates that the correlation between the SAT–Math and GPA is

r = .555. From this it is seen that r2 = .3080, which tells us that 30.80% of the variation in the SAT–Math scores can be accounted for by differences in the GPA scores. Now, should we worry about this? Not to panic!

Recall that inferential techniques which are used in testing mean differences require that numerous assumptions be met. Many times such assumptions cannot be satisfied in specific situations. For example, when one is examining a single dependent variable (response variable) with two factors (such as the example of the two–way ANOVA in this section), it is assumed that we have randomly assigned the AUs to the specific cells (factor A and factor B) and then the interventions or different conditions occur. Frequently such a random assignment is not possible. Under these conditions, it is useful to be able to adjust the values of the response variable for one or more independent variables which could not be controlled for. Once this adjustment has been made (and we let the software take care of that for us), then the standard analysis of variance can be accomplished to ascertain whether there are significant differences among average values of the response variable. This process is referred to as the **analysis of covariance** (*) or simply **ANCOVA** (*).

Now, let's apply this concept to the comparisons which we have just analyzed in relating the SAT–Math score to the number of honors level math courses taken and the sex of the student. We have seen that no significant differences have been found between the male and female students but the numbers of honors level courses taken clearly seems to relate to the average SAT–Math score attained. Suppose we ask the following questions: "What about the possible influence of the student's GPA on the average Math–Sat score?" "Might not the differences in average SAT–Math scores be accounted for by differences in the numbers of honors level math courses taken?" This is where the Analysis of Covariance methodology enters on the scene.

This software, as well as most other statistical software available today, allows us to first examine the relationship between the dependent variable (SAT–Math) and an independent, and possibly correlated, variable (in this case the GPA), referred to as the **covariate** (*). If such a relationship does exist then the methodology adjusts the dependent variable for this relationship and proceeds with the analysis of variance. Fortunately, the software utilized in this manual provides for a rapid approach to testing the hypothesis of no relationship, or correlation, between the dependent and independent variables, and then allows for an automatic adjustment of the dependent variable before the ANOVA is conducted. (**NOTE**: Caution must be exercised in using the Analysis of Covariance when the relationship between the dependent variable and the covariate are not statistically significant.)

Let us proceed with the example given in Exhibit 7.18 but include in our overall analysis the possibility that the GPA might have an influence on the response variable (the SAT–Math scores). Exhibit 7.21 summarizes this analysis.

EXHIBIT 7.21 RESULTS OF A COMPARISON AMONG SAT–MATH MEAN VALUES WHEN THE ANALYSIS UNIT IS CLASSIFIED BY THE NUMBER OF HONORS LEVEL MATH COURSES TAKEN AND THE SEX OF THE STUDENT, AND THE SAT–MATH SCORES ARE ADJUSTED FOR THE POSSIBLE CORRELATION WITH THE STUDENT'S GPA.

Analysis of Variance Report

Source	DF	Sum–Squares	Mean Square	F–Ratio	Prob>F
X(**GPA**)	1	60742.06	60742.06	10.13	**0.0015**
A (**SEX**)	1	14469.19	14469.19	2.41	**0.1203**
B (**MATHLVL**)	5	619111.7	123822.3	20.65	**0.0000**
AB	5	19151.22	3830.244	0.64	**0.6703**
ERROR	211	1265046	5995.479		
TOTAL(Adj)	223	3177384			

We should first notice that the row labeled X(**GPA**) shows a Prob value of 0.0015. The null hypothesis here is that there is no relationship (correlation) between the SAT–Math and the GPA. This hypothesis is rejected at $\alpha = .05$ with better than 99% confidence (1–0.0015 = 9985). We can, therefore, retain the assumed independent variable (GPA) in the analysis and proceed with tests of the hypotheses on the two main effects (sex and number of honors level math courses taken) and the interaction.

Let's again assume that we are using the .05 level of significance (risk). Considering the information in Exhibit 7.21, the following conclusions may be drawn with respect to the three hypotheses:

Null hypothesis A: There is no difference between the average SAT–Math score between males and females after adjusting for the GPA.

Statistical Findings, Hypothesis A: Since the Prob value of 0.1203 is greater than the α value of .05, the null hypothesis may not be rejected.

Conclusion A: What differences exist between male and female average SAT–Math scores are not large enough for us to be willing to conclude, with the confidence established, that we can reject the null hypothesis.

Null hypothesis B: There is no difference in average SAT–Math scores when taking into consideration the number of honors level math courses taken, after adjusting for the GPA.

Statistical Findings, Hypothesis B: Since the Prob value of 0.0000 is less than the α value of .05, the null hypothesis may be rejected.

Conclusion B: There is a difference in average SAT–Math scores among the students taking different numbers of honors level math courses, after adjusting for the GPA.

At this point the Fisher's LSD would be called for to identify among which number of honors level courses the average SAT–Math scores differ. Analysis of the differences using Fisher's LSD methodology yields the information in Exhibit 7.22 which indicates that the greater the number of honors level math courses a student takes, on average, the greater will be his or her average SAT–Math score. In addition, with the exception of students taking 0 and 1 honor level courses, which are not significantly different from each other (possibly due to the small sample size for the 0 level students), all other averages are significantly different at $\alpha = .05$. These findings are consistent with those reported earlier when the GPA was not considered as a covariate. Please note that things don't always work out the way we'd like or expect when applying inferential methods to the analysis of data.

EXHIBIT 7.22 A COMPARISON OF SAT–MATH AVERAGE SCORES USING FISHER'S LSD METHOD-OLOGY WHEN CONSIDERING THE NUMBER OF HONORS LEVEL MATH COURSES TAKEN, AFTER ADJUSTING FOR THE CORRELATION BETWEEN THE SAT–MATH SCORE AND GPA.

No. Honors Math Course (Code)*	Mean SAT–Math	LEVEL CODES* A B C D E F
0 (A)	320.5	. . S**S S S
1 (B)	378.4	. . S S S S
2 (C)	415.3	S S . S S S
3 (D)	462.5	S S S . S S
4 (E)	545.9	S S S S . S
5 (F)	605.8	S S S S S .

* Represents the assigned code associated with the specific number of honors level math courses taken.

** "S" indicates significant difference between row and column codes; "." indicates no significant difference.

Now, continuing with the interaction hypothesis, it is seen that:

Hypothesis AB: The main effects of Sex and number of honors level math courses do not provide an interaction effect on the average SAT–Math score, after adjusting for the GPA.

Statistical Findings, Hypothesis AB: Since the Prob value of 0.6703 is greater than the α value of .05, the null hypothesis cannot be rejected.

Conclusion AB: This does not mean that there are no differences in the populations. It only means that if differences exist they are sufficiently small that, based upon these samples, they were not considered statistically significant.

Up to this point in our discussion of hypothesis testing, we have considered a single dependent variable, which might be examined using one or more factors (often referred to as independent variables). We now move to examine hypothesis testing when we are considering two or more variables at the same time.

Testing Two or More Than Two Characteristics: Correlation and Regression; Discriminant Analysis

This section of this manual directs attention to issues associated with testing hypotheses when two or more characteristics (primary variables) are considered. In Chapter 6, the concept of relational measures was introduced. The discussion centered on developing descriptive statistics when there were two variables and again when there were more than two variables. Further, the distinction between correlation and regression was presented. Two databases, 2SCH4 and ENGSCO (See Appendices E and F, respectively), were used for the material which followed. These same two databases will be the source of the discussions that follow. At this time, the reader should review the descriptive statistics discussion in the section titled Relational Measures.

In addition to the concepts of correlation and regression, this section will also examine a new inferential technique referred to as **Discriminant Analysis** (*).

Two Variables: Correlation and Regression

First, we'll consider the issue of correlation between two variables, utilizing the ENGSCO database, and then we'll examine the same concepts for the 2SCH4 database. In Exhibit 7.23 are the correlations between all possible pairs of variables in the ENGSCO database.

EXHIBIT 7.23 A COMPARISON OF ALL POSSIBLE CORRELATION COEFFICIENTS IN THE
ENGSCO DATABASE*

	FRESHMKS	CAT	HS_GPA	ENG_PRE
FRESHMKS	1.000000	0.365899	0.669243	*0.544108*
CAT	0.365899	1.000000	0.432899	0.505623
HS_GPA	*0.669243*	0.432899	1.000000	0.526978
ENG_PRE	0.544108	0.505623	0.526978	1.000000

* Recall that the variables in this exhibit are:

        FreshMks: Freshman final English marks, a percentage

        CAT: a measure of aptitude, not necessarily an SAT score

        HS_GPA: the final high school grade point average

        ENG_Pre: a freshman English pre–test score, ranging from 0–50

In Exhibit 7.23, two correlation coefficients are highlighted, namely, Freshman marks with high school GPA (0.669243) and Freshman marks with the English Pre–Test score (0.544108). Recall that these numbers are referred to as the correlation coefficient or Pearson's Product Moment correlation coefficient. Recall also that the square of these numbers is referred to as the coefficient of determination and represents the proportion of variation in one variable that can be explained by the variation in the other variable. In this situation, it is seen that the respective coefficients of determination are:

Freshman marks high school GPA: r^2 $= (.669)^2 = .4476 = 44.76\%$

Freshman marks and English Pre–test: $r^2 = (.544)^2 = .2959 = 29.59\%$

Now, let's examine the relationship between the freshman marks and the high school GPA graphically, as in Exhibit 7.24.

EXHIBIT 7.24 A GRAPHIC COMPARISON OF FRESHMAN MARKS AND HIGH SCHOOL GRADE
POINT AVERAGE FOR THE ENGSCO DATABASE

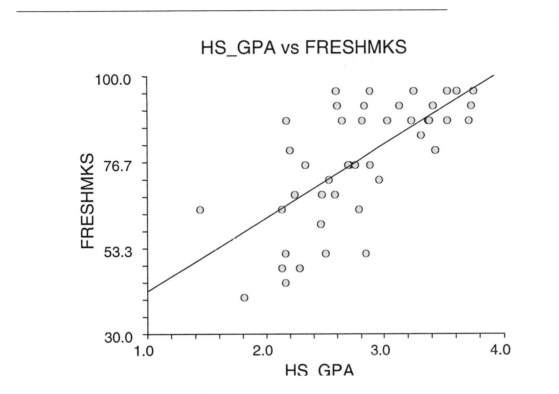

This visual certainly suggests a positive relationship between the two variables. Now, let's move into an inferential mode and, assuming that this is a sample from a large population, ask the following question:

> Is there a relationship (correlation) between freshman marks and high school grade point average in the population from which this sample has been selected?

This is our research question. Now, what might be an appropriate hypothesis? Right:

> There is no correlation between freshman marks and the high school grade point average, symbolically given as $\rho = 0$.

Our inferential procedure here makes it necessary to let the statistical software determine the probability of a correlation ($r = 0.669$) as large as this one occurring by chance alone if the null hypothesis were true. In this case, we shall assume an α of .05. The appropriate p value is seen to be .0000. (Please see the bold italicized number in Exhibit 7.25.) Therefore, we reject the null hypothesis with better than 95% confidence (in fact, we can state with 99.99% confidence) and conclude that there is a real correlation (i.e., different from 0) in the population from which this sample has been selected.

EXHIBIT 7.25 ANALYSIS INFORMATION TO TEST THE HYPOTHESIS OF NO CORRELATION BETWEEN FRESHMAN MARKS AND HIGH SCHOOL GPA

Independent Variable	Regression Coefficient	Standard Error	T-Value (Ho:ρ=0)	Prob Level	Decision (α= .05)
Intercept	***21.59243***	9.6309	2.242	0.030174	Reject Ho
HS_GPA	***20.01386***	3.3887	5.906	***0.000001***	Reject Ho
R-Squared	0.447886				

Recall that this same exhibit provides us with the regression equation which gives us the ability to estimate the freshman marks from high school grade point average. Data for the regression equation (See bold numbers in Exhibit 7.25) are seen to yield the following equation:

$$Y' = 21.59+20.01 \ X$$

where x is the high school GPA and Y' is the predicted freshman mark. For the bivariate (two variables) case, a rejection of no correlation also implies a rejection of the hypothesis that the slope of the regression equation is 0.

As is seen in Chapter 6, one can predict an expected freshman mark by selecting a GPA, say 2.0, in the above equation and calculating the expected Freshman Mark. In this case it is seen to be:

$$21.59+20.01 \ (2.0) = 61.61 \text{ or } 61.6$$

It is not the intent of this manual to discuss the prediction process further. However, the reader should be aware that each prediction by this process will have associated with it an error which is dependent upon the amount of correlation between the two variables as well as the sample size and confidence level selected. The greater the correlation, the smaller, in a relative sense, the error in estimation. (Please see references on multivariate analysis.)

Now, let's consider the 2SCH4 database. Exhibit 7.26 identifies the correlations between all possible combinations of five variables taken from this database.

EXHIBIT 7.26 A COMPARISON OF ALL POSSIBLE CORRELATION COEFFICIENTS OF FIVE VARIABLES IN THE 2SCH4 DATABASE*

	No SAT	SATVERB	SATMath	HonEng	GPA
No SAT	1.000000	0.162819	0.323179	0.180241	0.284636
SATVERB	0.162819	1.000000	***0.589085***	0.536336	***0.464038***
SATMath	0.323179	0.589085	1.000000	0.439337	0.555203
HonEng	0.180241	0.536336	0.439337	1.000000	0.536019
GPA	0.284636	0.464038	0.555203	0.536019	1.000000

* Recall that the variables in this exhibit are:

No SAT: number of times taking the SAT
SATVERB: SAT Verbal Score
SATMath: SAT Math Score
HonEng: number of honors level English courses taken
GPA: high school grade point average

In Exhibit 7.26, two correlations are highlighted:

SAT Verbal and SAT Math: r = .589085

SAT Verbal and GPA: r = .464038

The corresponding coefficients of determination are:

SAT Verbal and SAT Math: r^2 = .3470

SAT Verbal and GPA: r^2 = .2153

In Exhibit 7.26, the highest pairwise correlation is between the SAT Verbal and the SAT Math (0.589085), with the next highest correlation being between the SAT Math and the high school GPA (0.555203). For purposes of illustration, however, let's consider an analysis using the high school GPA as the independent variable and the SAT Verbal as the dependent variable. Exhibit 7.27 shows the scatter plot (*) between high school GPA and the SAT Verbal scores. Once again we see a positive relationship between the two variables identified in this exhibit.

EXHIBIT 7.27 A GRAPHIC COMPARISON OF HIGH SCHOOL GPA
AND SAT VERBAL SCORES FOR THE 2SCH4 DATABASE

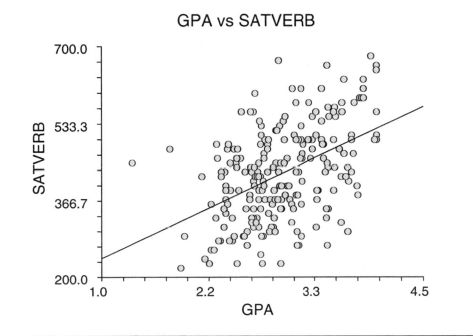

As in the previous illustration using the ENGSCO database, we will set up a research question:

Is there any relationship (correlation) between a student's high school grade point average and his/her SAT Verbal score?

We now know what the appropriate null hypothesis is:

There is no relationship between the high school grade point average and the SAT Verbal score, or ρ = 0.

In order to test this null hypothesis, we must use our statistical software and might possibly obtain a printout similar to Exhibit 7.28.

EXHIBIT 7.28 ANALYSIS INFORMATION TO TEST HYPOTHESIS OF NO CORRELATION BETWEEN HIGH SCHOOL GRADE POINT AVERAGE AND SAT VERBAL SCORES

Independent Variable	Regression Coefficient	Standard Error	T-Value (Ho: ρ = 0)	Prob Level	Decision (5%)
Intercept	146.8789	36.32602	4.0434	0.000053	Reject Ho
GPA	94.25654	12.07606	7.8052	*0.000000*	Reject No

If we establish the risk level (α) as .05, then we see that the p value (emphasized in Exhibit 7.28 in the column headed **Prob Level**) is less than the risk (α) and hence reject the null hypothesis with better than 95% confidence (actually better than 99.99%).

This same exhibit provides us with the data necessary to provide the regression equation from which a high school GPA may be used to predict an expected SAT Verbal score. This regression equation is determined from the values in the column headed **Regression Coefficient**, namely,

$$Y' = 146.88 + 94.26 X$$

where X is the high school GPA and Y' is the predicted SAT Verbal score. This equation suggests that, on average, an increase of 1 point in the GPA would bring about an expected increase in the SAT Verbal of 94.26 points. Another way to look at the prediction is that an increase of .1 in the GPA would bring about an expected increase in the SAT Verbal of 9.4 points (.1x94.26). Recall that the 146.88 is called the intercept, and the 94.26 is referred to as the slope of the regression line or the coefficient of X.

Let's consider what happens when we examine the possible relationship among more than one independent variable, the Xs, and the dependent variable, Y.

More Than Two Variables: Correlation and Regression

Now let's move into what is referred to as multiple regression or the multivariate case. Here there is a single dependent variable, but there is more than one possible independent variable. Since the ENGSCO database has only four variables, let's examine what might happen if we use three of the variables to predict the freshman mark. Exhibit 7.29 provides information for analysis, using freshman marks as the dependent variable and the other three variables as the independent variables. But first, let's consider two possible research questions:

Is there any relationship between the three independent variables and the freshman marks?

Are any of the independent variables significantly correlated with freshman marks?

What might be possible null hypotheses?

There is no relationship between the three independent variables and the freshman marks.

None of the independent variables is significantly correlated with the freshman marks.

While these null hypotheses seem relatively straightforward, let's ask the question, What happens if we reject the null hypothesis? A rejection of "None are significant" would seem to imply that some are (at least one is) significant, right?

EXHIBIT 7.29 ANALYSIS INFORMATION TO TEST THE HYPOTHESIS THAT NONE OF THE INDEPENDENT VARIABLES IS SIGNIFICANTLY CORRELATED WITH THE DEPENDENT VARIABLE, FRESHMAN MARKS.

Independent Variable	Regression Coefficient	Standard Error	T-Value (Ho: $\rho = 0$)	Prob Level	Decision (5%)
Intercept	21.56957	12.4945	1.7263	0.091818	Not reject Ho
CAT	.00324075	0.114171	0.0284	*0.977484*	Not reject Ho
HS_GPA	15.81134	3.995442	3.9573	*0.000294*	Reject Ho
ENG-Pre	0.5161603	0.273345	1.8883	*0.066074*	Not reject Ho
R-Squared	0.498632				

If we examine the bold italicized numbers in the column headed **Prob Level**, we see 0.977484, 0.000294 and 0.066074. Assuming we have selected the 0.5 level of significance, we would reject the null hypothesis for only the high school GPA (HS_GPA). Unlike previous tests of significance, we can expect to find one, two or more independent variables as significant contributors, or none at all. Our judgment is based upon the values in the **Prob Level** column. It should also be noted that we associate the **Prob Level** values with the labels in the column headed **Independent Variable**.

Ordinarily one might stop at this point, discard the two non-significant variables and recalculate the regression equation using only the high school GPA. However, because the "independent" variables are not truly independent (See the correlation matrix in Exhibit 7.26), the author of this manual uses an "invented" algorithm when the 5% level has been selected, namely:

If the **Prob Level** value for any of the independent variables lies between .05 and .10, include that variable in the recalculation of the regression equation.

A similar algorithm would apply if the level of significance was .01.

It might be of interest to note what the regression equation and the multiple coefficient of determination would have been if all of the three independent variables were significant:

$$Y' = 21.57 = .0032*(CAT) = 15.81*(HS\_GPA) = 0.516*(ENG\_PRE)$$

where the * symbol means to multiply the numerical term by the specific value for the independent variables.

It should also be noted that Exhibit 7.29, as well as earlier exhibits which are used in regression analysis, provides us with the estimate for the multiple coefficient of determination, namely:

$$R^2 = 0.498632$$

Now, recognizing that we should exclude the CAT variable from the analysis due to the large value of the Prob Level, we will let our software recalculate the information in Exhibit 7.29 but with the CAT scores not included in the analysis. The resulting analysis information is seen in Exhibit 7.30.

EXHIBIT 7.30 ANALYSIS INFORMATION TO TEST THE HYPOTHESIS THAT NEITHER OF TWO INDEPENDENT VARIABLES IS SIGNIFICANTLY CORRELATED WITH THE DEPENDENT VARIABLE, FRESHMAN MARKS

Independent Variable	Regression Coefficient	Standard Error	T-Value (Ho: $\rho = 0$)	Prob Level	Decision (5%)
Intercept	21.80332	9.286906	2.3477	0.023673	Reject Ho
HS_GPA	15.8371	3.844573	4.1193	*0.000174*	Reject Ho
ENG-Pre	0.5189717	0.251735	2.0616	*0.045472*	Reject Ho
R-Squared	0.498622				

If we examine the bold italicized numbers in the **Prob Level** column and assume we are still using an α of .05, we see that the high school GPA has a value of .000174, and the English pre-test has a value of .045472. It should be clear from this that the high school GPA remains significant with better than 95% confidence, and the English pre-test score now becomes significant with slightly better than 95% confidence. So, from this analysis we can conclude that the regression equation for predicting the SAT Verbal from the high school GPA and the English pre-test scores is given by the terms in the column headed **Independent Variable**, namely:

$$Y' = 21.80+15.84*(HS\_GPA)+.519*(ENG-PRE)$$

where again the * means to multiply the specific coefficient by the specific value for the high school GPA and the English pre-test.

We should also note that the multiple coefficient of determination is given by:

$$R^2 = 0.498622$$

Let's suppose that a student has a high school GPA of 3.0 and an English pre-test score of 45. What would his or her predicted freshman English mark be? If we substitute these two values in the above equation, we have:

$$Y' = 21.80+15.84*(HS\_GPA)+.519*(ENG\_PRE)$$

$$Y' = 21.80 + 15.84*(3.0) + .519*(45)$$

$$Y' = 21.80 + 47.52 + 20.76 = 90.08$$

Recall that this is the expected freshman English mark and that there will be an error associated with this estimate, the magnitude of the error depending upon the extent of the correlation among the variables, the sample size and the confidence level one selects.

Now, before proceeding to examine the data from the 2SCH4 database, let's summarize our findings for the three regression situations, which we have considered. This information may be found in Exhibit 7.31.

EXHIBIT 7.31 A COMPARISON OF THREE REGRESSION ANALYSES FOR DATA FROM THE ENGSCO DATABASE WHEN THE FRESHMAN ENGLISH MARK IS THE DEPENDENT VARIABLE

Regression Equation	Coefficient of Determination
Y' = 21.59 + 20.01*(HS_GPA)	0.4479
Y' = 21.57 + 15.81*(HS_GPA) + 0.516(ENG_PRE) + .0032*(CAT)	0.4986
Y" = 21.80 + 15.84*(HS_GPA) + 0.519(ENG_PRE)	0.4986

From the data in Exhibit 7.31, the following observations can be made:

1. The coefficient of determination increases from 0.4479 to 0.4986 when the English pre-test and the CAT scores are added as independent variables to the high school GPA.

2. When there is an indication that the CAT scores do not contribute significantly to predicting the expected freshman English mark and the CAT scores are removed from the analysis, the coefficient of determination remains at 0.4986. This clearly indicates that the CAT scores add nothing to explaining the variability of the freshman English marks.

3. The fact that the CAT is not significant in predicting the freshman English marks is evident in examining the last two regression equations in Exhibit 7.31 where the intercept changes only slightly, the high school GPA coefficient is virtually identical and the English pre-test coefficient is the same.

4. The major shift in value occurs in the coefficient of the high school GPA when the English pre-test is added as an independent variable. This GPA coefficient changes from 20.01 to 15.81.

Changes in intercepts, independent variable coefficients and the coefficient of determination will provide the user of this multiple regression procedure with an ability to seek out reasons for differences in (or the variability of) the dependent variable.

Now let's move on to an examination of data from the 2SCH4 database. For purposes of the analyses, which follow, Exhibit 7.26 is reproduced below as Exhibit 7.32 but with the SAT Math removed as a variable of interest.

EXHIBIT 7.32 A COMPARISON OF CORRELATION COEFFICIENTS OF FOUR VARIABLES IN THE 2SCH4 DATABASE*

	No SAT	SATVERB	HonEng	GPA
No SAT	1.000000	0.162819	0.180241	0.284636
SATVERB	0.162819	1.000000	0.536336	0.464038
HonEng	0.180241	0.536336	1.000000	0.536019
GPA	0.284636	0.464038	0.536019	1.000000

* Recall that the variables in this exhibit are:
 No SAT: number of times taking the SAT
 SATVERB: SAT Verbal score
 HonEng: number of honors level English courses taken
 GPA: high school grade point average

Let us further assume that we are interested in predicting the SAT Verbal score based upon the number of times taking the SAT (No SAT), the number of honors level English courses taken (HonEng) and the high school GPA (GPA). Exhibits 7.33, 7.34 and 7.35 present a visual impression of the relationship between the independent variables, one at a time, and the dependent variable SAT Verbal scores.

EXHIBIT 7.33 A GRAPHIC COMPARISON OF NUMBER OF TIMES TAKING THE SAT AND SAT VERBAL SCORES FOR THE 2SCH4 DATABASE

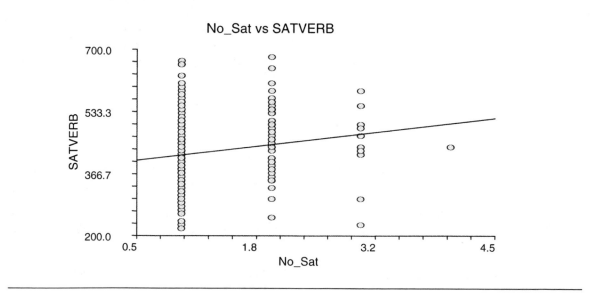

EXHIBIT 7.34 A GRAPHIC COMPARISON OF NUMBER OF HONORS LEVEL ENGLISH COURSES
TAKEN AND SAT VERBAL SCORES FOR THE 2SCH4 DATABASE

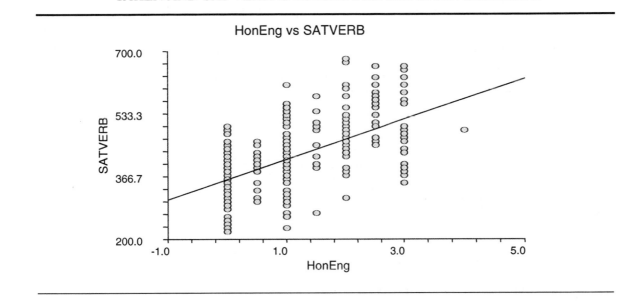

EXHIBIT 7.35 A GRAPHIC COMPARISON OF HIGH SCHOOL GPA
AND SAT VERBAL SCORES FOR THE 2SCH4 DATABASE

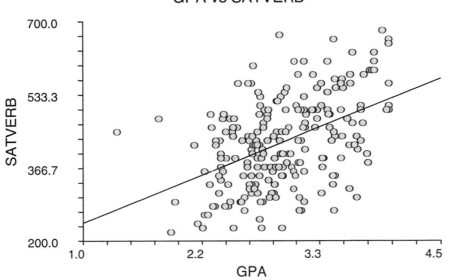

From these three graphs, it appears that there is a positive relationship between the SAT Verbal and the number of honors level English courses taken (Exhibit 7.34) and the high school GPA (Exhibit 7.35). However, the relationship between the SAT Verbal scores and the number of times taking the SAT (Exhibit 7.33) appears to be the smallest. This visual impression is supported by the lowest correlation coefficient as given in exhibit 7.32, namely: 0.1628.

Recall earlier in this chapter that the bivariate regression equation, where the independent variable is high school GPA and the dependent variable is SAT Verbal, was given by the expression:

$$Y' = 146.88 + 94.26\ X$$

This equation was found to be significant with better than 99.99% confidence. Now, let's move into the multiple regression or multivariate analysis case for the 2SCH4 database. Let's assume that our three independent variables of interest are:

> Number of times taking the SAT
> Number of honors level English courses taken
> High School GPA

Now, let's consider two possible research questions:

> Is there any relationship between the SAT Verbal and the three independent variables?

> Are any of the independent variables significantly correlated with the SAT Verbal scores?

Now, what might be possible null hypotheses? Right!

> There is no relationship between the SAT Verbal scores and the three independent variables.

> None of the independent variables is significantly correlated with the SAT Verbal scores.

Recall that we must consider what happens if we reject the null hypothesis. What question arises? A rejection of the null hypothesis would imply that at least one of the independent variables is significant. Our question, therefore, is, which one or ones? Let's consider the information in Exhibit 7.36.

EXHIBIT 7.36 ANALYSIS INFORMATION TO TEST THE HYPOTHESIS THAT NONE OF THE INDEPENDENT VARIABLES IS SIGNIFICANTLY CORRELATED WITH THE DEPENDENT VARIABLE, SAT VERBAL SCORE

Independent Variable	Regression Coefficient	Standard Error	T-Value (Ho: $\rho = 0$)	Prob Level	Decision (5%)
Intercept	224.6647	36.23698	6.1999	.000000	Reject Ho
No SAT	3/705119	9.995861	0.3707	*0.710887*	Non-Rej Ho
HonEng	40.24744	6.527962	6.1654	*0.000000*	Reject Ho
GPA	49.17647	13.61374	3.6123	*0.000304*	Reject Ho
R-squared	0.331810				

If we examine the bold italicized numbers in the column headed **Prob Level**, we see the values 0.710887, 0.000000 and 0.000304. Assuming that we have selected the .05 level of significance, it follows that the independent variable No SAT (number of times taking the SAT) is not a significant contributor to our prediction of the SAT Verbal score. The variables HonEng (number of honors level English courses taken) and GPA are, however, significant at considerably better than the .05 level. Again, we note that the values in the **Prob Level** column are associated with the variables in the column headed **Independent Variable**.

Note that what we have done is to not reject the null hypothesis with respect to the No SAT variable but to reject the null hypothesis with respect to the HonEng and GPA variables.

Now, recognizing that we should exclude the No SAT independent variable from the analysis, we repeat the process using our statistical software but with the No SAT variable excluded from the analysis. The resulting analysis information is seen in Exhibit 7.37.

EXHIBIT 7.37 ANALYSIS INFORMATION TO TEST THE HYPOTHESIS THAT NEITHER OF TWO INDEPENDENT VARIABLES IS SIGNIFICANTLY CORRELATED WITH THE DEPENDENT VARIABLE, FRESHMAN MARKS

Independent Variable	Regression Coefficient	Standard Error	T-Value (Ho: $\beta = 0$)	Prob Level	Decision (5%)
Intercept	226.0991	35.95937	6.2876	0.000000	Reject Ho
HonEng	40.33017	6.511401	6.1938	*0.000000*	Reject Ho
GPA	50.31907	13.23425	3.8022	*0.000143*	Reject Ho
R-squared	0.331393				

Again, the overall null hypothesis is that none of the independent variables is significantly correlated with the dependent variable. Viewing the bold italicized values in the column headed **Prob Level**, we see that the HonEng and GPA are significant with better than 99.9% confidence. So, from this analysis, we can conclude that the regression equation which provides us with two statistically significant independent variables is given by the expression:

$$Y' = 226.10 + 40.33 * (HonEng) + 50.32 * (GPA)$$

where again the * means to multiply the specific coefficients by the specific values for the HonEng and GPA variables.

and the multiple coefficient of determination is seen to be:

$$R^2 = 0.331393$$

Let's suppose that a high school student has taken four honors level English courses with an associated GPA of 3.2. What might be the predicted SAT Verbal score? Let's substitute these values in the above equation.

$$Y' = 226.10 + 40.33 * (4) + 50.32 * (3.2)$$

$$Y' = 226.10 + 161.32 + 161.02$$

$$Y' = 548.44$$

Recall that this is the expected SAT Verbal score and that there will be an error associated with this estimate, the magnitude of the error depending upon the extent of the correlation among the variables, the sample size and the confidence level one selects.

Now, let's summarize our findings from the three analyses which we have performed on the 2SCH4 database. This information can be found in Exhibit 7.38.

EXHIBIT 7.38 A COMPARISON OF THREE REGRESSION ANALYSES FOR DATA FROM THE 2SCH4 DATABASE WHEN THE SAT VERBAL SCORE IS THE DEPENDENT VARIABLE

Regression Equation	R^2
Y' = 146.88 + 94.26*(GPA)	0.2153
Y' = 224.66 + 49.18*(GPA) + 40.25*(HonEng) + 3.71*(NoSAT)	0.3318
Y' = 226.10 + 50.32*(GPA) + 40.33*(HonEng)	0.3314

From the data in Exhibit 7.38, the following observations can be made:

1. The coefficient of determination (R^2) ranges from 0.2153 when the single independent variable is GPA to 0.3318 when there are three independent variables, namely, GPA, number of honors English courses taken and number of times taking the SAT.

2. When the number of times taking the SAT is eliminated as a non-significant independent variable, the coefficient of determination drops from 0.3318 to 0.3314. In other words, the number of times taking the SAT contributes little or nothing to explaining the variation in the SAT Verbal scores.

3. While there are big differences in the intercept and the individual slopes from the single GPA independent variable regression equation (first line in the exhibit above) to only two independent variables (third line in the exhibit above), the differences in the intercepts and slopes in the regression line including the number of times taking the SAT and the regression line without this independent variable are only slight. This is consistent with the analysis which eliminated the number of times taking the SAT as a significant independent variable.

Changes in intercepts, independent variable coefficients and the coefficient of determination will provide the user of this multiple regression procedure with an ability to seek out reasons for differences in (or the variability of) the dependent variable.

The reader should understand that multiple (multivariate) regression analysis is quite complex and should be used with caution when a large number of "independent" variables are employed. Several references are given on multiple regression later in this manual.

Discriminant Analysis

Another approach to multivariate analysis which might be quite useful to the researcher is referred to as **discriminant analysis** (*). It is the intent of this section of the manual to acquaint the researcher with the usefulness of discriminant analysis as a research tool rather than present some of the more complicated statistical procedures associated with this approach.

First, a discussion of several examples where discriminant analysis may be useful.

EXAMPLE A: Imagine that you are director of a program at an institution of higher education, perhaps at the masters or doctorate level. You have become concerned over the increasing numbers of students who do not complete the program. In your search for reasons behind this increase, you have decided to look at characteristics associated with your students, both those who complete the program and those who don't. You develop a list of these characteristics, such as age at time of entry, high school GPA, bachelors GPA, GRE score and gross income. Your question: Which, if any, of these characteristics might be useful in predicting whether a future applicant for the program would be likely to complete the program? In other words, which characteristics, if any, would serve to discriminate between those who complete the program and those who do not. This situation calls for the use of discriminant analysis as one possible methodological approach.

EXAMPLE B: Imagine that you are a high school counselor and you would like to determine whether any characteristics of your students could be helpful in identifying which students might successfully complete their four years of college. Possible characteristics might be grade point average through the junior year, an SAT Verbal score, an SAT Math score, the number of honors level courses taken in English, the number of non-athletic extra–curricular activities participated in and the number of athletic extra-curricular activities participated in. With these characteristics, and possibly others, the question being posed might be, "Which of these characteristics might help me as a counselor in advising students about their likelihood of success in (graduation from) college?" This situation calls for the use of discriminant analysis as one possible methodological approach.

EXAMPLE C: In developing a program for individuals who are arrested for driving under the influence (DUI), it is essential to assess whether there are characteristics of those arrested which might be related to whether or not they become repeat offenders (referred to as recidivists). Assume that we could identify a set of possible characteristics associated with those arrested as DUIs. Assume further that we can classify those arrested as repeaters and non-repeaters. The question we might ask is, "Which of these identified characteristics might possibly serve to discriminate between those likely to be repeat offenders and those not likely to repeat?" This situation calls for the use of discriminant analysis as one possible methodological approach.

The process involves submitting the set of possible discriminating characteristics to a statistical procedure similar to the previously discussed multiple regression. This procedure enables the researcher to discard characteristics which do not either significantly (from a statistical perspective) differentiate between the two categories (succeed versus fail) or do not satisfy some set of probability for discriminating successfully. Caution: in practice, no discrimination process is perfect. As in rejection and non-rejection, so we will find missclassifying individuals into the wrong category part of the time.

The process involves the calculation of a discriminant equation, such as:

$$Y' = b_1X_1 + b_2X_2 + B_3X_3 + ...$$

where the bs are analogous to the slopes in the regression equations and the Xs represent the particular characteristics which are deemed capable of aiding in the discrimination process. The value for Y is used to predict whether the individual analysis unit (AU) falls into one of the two categories. Fortunately, available statistical software makes this process considerably less tedious than it was many years ago.

One final point, the discriminant analysis process also makes it possible to discriminate among more than two categories.

Selected Nonparametric Procedures

In this final section of the manual, a number of nonparametric or distribution-free statistical procedures are presented. Several excellent references are given later in this manual, should the reader desire to pursue specific analyses in greater detail. First of all, let's discuss what makes these methods nonparametric or distribution-free.

With the exception of the chi-square test presented earlier in this chapter, all other methods of analysis assume something about the form of the distribution(s) and the parameters of the distribution(s). For example, in the one-way analysis of variance where we are testing a hypothesis about two samples, we are assuming that the samples are drawn from populations with the same mean (μ) and standard deviation (σ) and that the distributions are normally distributed. In many of the other analyses, assumptions are made that the errors associated with the analyses are normally distributed with means = 0 and common standard deviations. In each of these situations, we speak of performing a **parametric analysis** (*) since we make assumptions about the form of the distribution as well as values of the parameters, such as the arithmetic mean and standard deviation.

Nonparametric (*) or **distribution-free** (*) statistical methods on the other hand make no assumptions about values of the parameters or the forms of the distributions. It is pointed out in Marascuilo & McSweeney (1977) that Bradley (1968) does make a distinction between the two statistical methods. (Please see the Glossary in Appendix D for this distinction.) In this section, we will refer to the methodology as nonparametric only.

Now, let's proceed to consider several of these methods.

The Sign Test

This test is often referred to as the granddaddy of all nonparametric tests. Let's consider a situation in which an instructor in statistics is interested in whether learning has taken place between a first and second quiz. The first quiz consists of 10 items. The second quiz consists of five items similar to some on the first quiz an five new items or topics. The instructor codes the students by the last four digits of their Social Security numbers and then records a grade for the first quiz and a grade on the second quiz for the appropriate five items testing concepts similar to those of the first quiz. Of interest to the instructor is whether his/her teaching between the two quizzes has reinforced or improved learning of the topics covered on the first quiz. The measure of learning is based upon whether the grade for the first five items of the second quiz is higher than the grade for the first quiz when grades are converted to a percentage.

The null hypothesis might be that the observed differences in percentage change are randomly distributed (i.e., half of the students improved and half did not). A rejection of this hypothesis, hopefully, would support the instructor's view that learning had occurred. One might compare this procedure to the tossing of a coin. Suppose an instructor had 20 students. In tossing a coin 20 times, one would expect, on average, 10 heads and 10 tails. The same notion would apply when looking at the change in the grades of the 20 students.

If there were no change, one might expect 10 students to have a negative percentage change and 10 to have a positive percentage change. This test procedure considers the number of cases in the positive and in the negative category and develops a **p** value under the assumption that no change has occurred.

The Wilcoxen (Mann-Whitney)

When a one-way analysis of variance is used to test the hypothesis of no difference in the means of populations from which two samples were drawn, there are assumptions made about the distributions of the two populations, namely, that the residuals are normally distributed with the variance everywhere the same. When such assumptions are deemed inappropriate, this nonparametric procedure may be employed. Consider the situation which follows.

Ten individuals enrolled in a graduate program at a well-known university are required to participate in a project which involves timing the length of time it takes to complete a task. Assume that the individuals have been classified into two age categories: those less than 40 years and those 40 years of age and older. Assume further that the variable of interest is time in seconds to complete the task. Exhibit 7.39 indicates the results.

EXHIBIT 7.39 TIME IN SECONDS TO COMPLETE A TASK WHEN
CONSIDERING TWO AGE GROUPINGS OF THE PARTICIPANTS

Less than 40 years of age	40 years of age or older
56 seconds (9)	59 seconds (8)
62 (6)	75 (3)
37 (10)	68 (5)
60 (7)	81 (2)
	74 (4)
	83 (1)

NOTE: Numbers in parentheses represent the rank associated with the
individual times, with the longest time having a rank of 1.

Now, what might be a null hypothesis in this situation? Right! The average number of seconds to accomplish the task is the same for the two age groups. However, in this procedure, the data are ranked and then the hypothesis modified as follows:

The average rank to accomplish the task is the same for the two groups.

The Kruskal-Wallis Test

This nonparametric procedure is analogous to a one-way analysis of variance when there are more than two categories of the single factor examined. To illustrate, suppose in the previous example the participants were classified into three age categories: less than 35, 35 to 45 and more than 45. A possible set of results might appear as in Exhibit 7.40.

EXHIBIT 7.40 TIME IN SECONDS TO COMPLETE A TASK
WHEN CONSIDERING THREE AGE GROUPINGS OF THE PARTICIPANTS

Less than 35 years of age	35 to 45 years of age	More than 45 years of age
56 seconds (11)	49 seconds (14)	59 seconds (10)
62 (7)	52 (13)	75 (3)
37 (15)	61 (8)	68 (5)
60 (9)	67 (6)	81 (2)
	53 (12)	74 (4)
		84 (1)

NOTE: Numbers in parentheses represent the rank associated with the
individual times, with the longest time having a rank of 1.

A possible null hypothesis, recognizing that we are converting the times to seconds to ranks, might be:

> There is no difference in average rank among the three age groups with respect to the accomplishment of a given task.

A rejection of this hypothesis clearly suggests that the three age group samples could not have come from the same population or from populations with the same distribution.

The McNemar Test

This particular test is useful when comparing frequencies on a dichotomous characteristic (such as Yes/No, Positive/Negative, or Support/Oppose) for the same individuals on different items at the same time or on the same item at different times. To illustrate, consider a situation in which an organization conducts a study, sampling from a population, on attitudes about certain issues and records these attitudes as either Support or Oppose. An assessment of the results suggests that the group being analyzed is not supportive of a specific issue. So, a campaign is mounted to better inform this group on reasons why the issue should be supported. Following this campaign, the same sample is again asked whether they Support or Oppose the issue, with the following possible results:s

EXHIBIT 7.41 A COMPARISON OF SUPPORT OR OPPOSE FOR A SPECIFIC ISSUE
AT TWO DIFFERENT POINTS IN TIME FOR THE SAME SAMPLE

FIRST SAMPLING	SECOND SAMPLING		
	SUPPORT	OPPOSE	FIRST SAMPLE TOTAL
SUPPORT	25	10	35
OPPOSE	50	15	65
SECOND SAMPLE TOTAL	75	25	100

If we examine the table carefully, we can make the following statements:

1. The sample size consists of 100 persons

2. On the first sampling, 35 supported the issue and 65 opposed the issue.

3. On the second sampling, 75 supported the issue and 25 opposed the issue.

4. Of those who supported the issue initially, 25 still support the issue, but 10 now oppose the issue.

5. Of those who opposed the issue initially, 15 still oppose the issue, but 50 now support the issue.

Now what might be a logical question to ask? Right:

Has there been a significant shift during the campaign from opposition to the issue to support of the issue?

This nonparametric procedure provides us with the ability to examine this question, testing the hypothesis that there has been no shift in opinions. A rejection of this hypothesis then calls for the researcher to examine the data and determine in which direction the shift has occurred.

Suppose there are more than two alternatives to an item which is asked two different times. This leads us to the next nonparametric procedure.

The Bowker Test

As an illustration, suppose that the options in assessing opinions are Support, Neither Support nor Oppose and Oppose. Suppose that on an initial sampling, a large number of respondents appear to be "on the fence." A campaign is mounted and the survey again taken on the same sample with the results for the two surveys appearing as in Exhibit 7.41.

EXHIBIT 7.42 A COMPARISON OF SUPPORT, NEITHER SUPPORT NOR OPPOSE AND OPPOSE FOR A SPECIFIC ISSUE AT TWO DIFFERENT POINTS IN TIME FOR THE SAME SAMPLE.

FIRST SAMPLING	SECOND SAMPLING		
	SUPPORT	NEITHER SUPPORT NOR OPPOSE	OPPOSE	FIRST SAMPLE TOTAL
SUPPORT	25	10	10	45
NEITHER SUPPORT NOR OPPOSE	60	10	10	80
OPPOSE	50	10	15	75
SECOND SAMPLE TOTAL	135	30	35	200

Now, if we examine Exhibit 7.42, we can make the following statements:

1. The sample consists of 200 persons.

2. Of the first sampling, 45 supported the issue, 80 neither supported nor opposed the issue, and 75 opposed the issue.

3. Of the second sampling, 135 supported the issue (a big shift), 30 neither supported nor opposed the issue, and 35 opposed the issue.

4. The big shift is seen from the Neither Support Nor Oppose responses from the first sampling (80 persons) to 135 persons supporting the issue in the second sampling.

5. Of these 80 who initially neither supported nor opposed the issue, 60 now support the issue.

6. Of the 75 who initially opposed the issue, 50 now support the issue.

Now, what might be a logical question to ask? Right!

Has there been a significant shift of opinions on this issue during the campaign?

This nonparametric procedure allows us to test the hypothesis of no change. However, unlike the McNemar procedure where the shift, if significant, is easy to identify, this analysis takes greater care because the shift may occur in a number of ways. The respondents who remained the same are the 25 who support, the 10 who neither support nor oppose and the 15 who oppose the issue. (Note the shaded items in Exhibit 7.42 on the main diagona). All others (unshaded and off the main diagonal) have changed their opinions.

The Kolmogorov-Smirnov Test

Suppose we have scores on a college entrance examination for students from two different locations. While interest frequently centers on whether there is a significant difference in the mean scores between the two groups, one might also be interested in examining whether the distributions were similar, that is, whether the two samples could have come from the same population or from populations having the same distribution. The null hypothesis, of course, would be either of the following two statements:

The two samples were drawn from the same population.

There is no difference in the distribution of the variable of interest in the populations from which the two samples were drawn.

Notice that this procedure says nothing about the form of the population distribution(s) and, hence, falls into the nonparametric category of inferential procedures.

*   *   *   *   *   *

And this ends our journey through some basics of descriptive and inferential statistics. The reader with greater interest in many of the topics covered in this manual should consult some of the excellent references contained in the bibliography/reference section of this manual. Perhaps browsing through this manual has given the reader an awareness of the subject and provided him or her with enough knowledge to be a questioning user and reviewer of statistical materials.

REFERENCES

Brase, C.H. & Brase, C.P. 1991). **Understandable statistics, 4th Edition**. Lexington, mA: D.C. Heath.

Cleveland, W.S. (1990). **Visualization: the new frontier of data analysis**. Summit, NJ: Hobart Press.

Couch, J.V. (1987) **Fundamentals of statistics for the behavioral science**. St. Paul, MN: West Publishing Company.

Crossen, Cynthia (1994) **Tainted Truth**. New York: Simon & Schuster.

Gibbons, J. D. (1993) **Nonparametric statistics, an introduction**. Quantitative Applications in the Social Sciences, Vol. 90. Thousand Oaks, CA: Sage Publications.

Gonick, L.& Smith, W. (1993) **The cartoon guide to statistics**. New York: HarperCollins Publishers.

Heiman, G. (1996). **Basic statistics for the behavioral sciences** (2nd ed.). Boston, MA: Houghton Mifflin Company.

Henry, G. T. (1995) **Graphing data, techniques for display and analysis**. Applied Social Research Methods Series, Volume 36. Thousand Oaks, CA: Sage Publications.

Hinkle, D.E., Wiersma, W., & Jurs, S.G. (1988) **Applied statistics for the behavioral** sciences (2nd ed.). Boston, MA: Houghton Mifflin Company

Hintz, J., (1998) **NCSS 2000**. Kaysville, Utah: NCSS Press.

Holcomb, Z.C. (1992). **Interpreting basic statistics**. Los Angeles, CA: Pyrczak Publishing.

Holcomb, Z.C. (1998). **Fundamentals of descriptive statistics**. Los Angeles, CA: Pyrczak Publishing.

Huck, S.W. and Cormier, W.H. (1996) **Reading statistics and research, 2nd Edition**. New York, NY: HarperCollins.

Huff, D. (1954). **How to lie with statistics**. New York: W. W. Norton

Isaac S. & Michael, W.B. (1995). **Handbook in research and evaluation, 3rd Edition**. San Diego, CA: EdITS Publishers.

Iverson, G.R., & Norpoth, H. (1987). **Analysis of variance**. Quantitative Applications in the Social Sciences, Vol. 1. Thousand Oaks, CA: Sage Publications.

Klecka, W. R. (1980) **Discriminant analysis.** Quantitative Applications in the Social Sciences, Vol. 19. Thousand Oaks, CA: Sage Publications.

Knapp, T. R. (1996) **Learning statistics through playing cards**. Thousand Oaks, CA: Sage Publications.

Kubiszyn, T. & Borich, G. (1987). **Educational testing and measurement**. Glenview, ILL: Scott, Foresman and Company.

Lewis-Beck, M. S. (1995) **Data analysis, an introduction.** Quantitative Applications in the Social Sciences, Vol. 103. Thousand Oaks, CA: Sage Publications.

Marascuilo, L. A., & McSweeney, M. (1977) **Nonparametric and distribution-free methods for the social sciences**. Monterey, CA: Brooks/Cole Publishing Company.

McCall, C.H. (1960). Linear contrasts, Parts I, II, and III. **Industrial Quality Control, July, August, September**, 19–21, 12–16, and 5–8.

McCall, C.H. (1982). **Sampling and statistics handbook for research**. Ames, Iowa: The Iowa State University Press.

McCall, C.H. (1999). **Understanding statistical methods, a manual for students and data analysts**. Culver City, CA: Personal.

Mohr, L.B. (1990) **Understanding significance testing.** Quantitative Applications in the Social Sciences, Vol. 73. Thousand Oaks, CA: Sage Publications.

Moore, D.S., & McCabe, G.P. (1989). **Introduction to the practice of statistics.** New York: W.H. Freeman and Company.

National Education Association, Research Division. (1992). **Status of the American public school teacher**. Washington, D.C.

Paulos, J.A. (1990). **Innumeracy**. New York, NY: Vantage Books.

Paulos, J.A. (1996). **A mathematician reads the newspaper**. New York, NY: Anchor Books, Doubleday

Quantitative Applications in the Social Sciences, A series of Papers. Thousand Oaks, CA: Sage Publications.

Schroeder, L.D., et al. (1986). **Understanding regression analysis, an introductory guide.** Quantitative Applications in the Social Sciences, Vol. 57. Thousand Oaks, CA: Sage Publications.

Siegel, S., & Castellan, J. (1988) **Nonparametric statistics for the behavioral sciences (2nd ed.).** New York: McGraw-Hill.

Szoka, K. (1983). Displaying concepts graphically: What chart should you use? **Small Business** Computers May/June.

Tufte, E. R. (1983) **The visual display of quantitative information**. Cheshire, CN: Graphics Press.

Tufte, E. R. (1990) **Envisioning information**. Cheshire, CN: Graphics Press.

Tufte, E.R. (1998). **Visual explanations**. Cheshire, CN: Graphics Press.

Vogt, W. P. (1993) **Dictionary of statistics and methodology.** Newbury Park, CA: Sage Publications.

Weinberg, S., & Goldberg, K. (1990) **Statistics for the behavioral sciences.** Cambridge: Cambridge University Press.

Wildt, A.R., & Ahtola, O.T. (1978). **Analysis of covariance.** Quantitative Applications in the Social Sciences, Vol. 12. Thousand Oaks, CA: Sage Publications.

APPENDIX A

SOME BASIC ARITHMETIC NOTATIONS

NOTATION	INTERPRETATION
X	Value of a characteristic
Σ	Summation sign; means "add up all that follows." The Greek letter capital sigma.
$\sqrt{X}$	Take the square root of X.
$X^{\frac{1}{2}}$	Take the square root of X.
X^{-1}	Take the reciprocal of X.
ΣX	Add the values of X.
ΣX^2	Square the values of X and then add them.
$(\Sigma X)^2$	Add the values for X and then square the total.
$[\Sigma(X - \mu)^2]^{\frac{1}{2}}$	Subtract the population mean from each observation; square each of these differences; add up the results; then take the square root of the result.

APPENDIX B

ELEMENTARY PROBABILITY

Samples for use in studies may be selected in a number of ways, and several were described in Chapter 3 of this text. There are yet other sampling procedures, such as judgment selection, purposive selection, incidental selection, haphazard selection and selection by volunteers. Under the right conditions any of these sampling methods will yield reasonably accurate estimates of parameters in the populations being sampled, but seldom can the researcher be certain that the conditions are right. There is virtually no way of knowing how accurate such estimates are, short of taking a census of the whole population. Even if a census were taken to verify an estimate made under one set of conditions, there is no guarantee of similar successes under different circumstances.

The only type of sample selection with mathematical properties that will permit calculation of the precision, or confidence limits, of sample estimates is *probability sampling*. A probability sample is one selected in accordance with a probability model for which it is possible to state in advance of selecting the sample (a) the probability that any given population analysis unit will be included in the sample and (b) the relationship of this probability to the probabilities for all other population elements.

A *probability model* is a sampling plan or sampling design in which specific probabilities are assigned for choosing analysis units to be included in the sample. In their complexity, probability models may vary from simple random sample to complicated multistage sample designs. The complexity of the design does not destroy its usefulness as a probability model; it only complicates the procedures for selecting the sample and, subsequently, for analyzing data obtained from the sample. On the other hand, the simplest design cannot serve as a probability model unless the probability that the analysis units are to be selected can be stated specifically.

Some Aspects of Probability

Probability is generally the ratio of the number of ways in which can event can succeed (or fail) to the number of ways in which it can occur. Suppose there are 1,000 slips of paper, numbered 1 to 1,000, in a bowl. What is the probability that the slip number 863 will be selected on the first draw? If the slips are well shuffled so that chance is the only factor affecting the selection, then the probability is 1 in 1,000, 1:1,000, or 1/1,000.

Instead of slips of paper, suppose 250 blue beads, 250 red beads and 500 white beads are placed in a bowl. What is the probability of drawing a blue bead on the first try? The probability would be 250/1000 or ¼ or 0.25. The numerator of the ratio, then, is the number of outcomes favorable to a specific event and the denominator is the number of possible outcomes.

Every probability may also be expressed as a proportion, usually a decimal with the base (or total) of 1.00. Thus, the probability of drawing slip number 863 from the 1,000 slips of paper in the bowl would be 1 in 1,000 or 0.001. The probability of drawing a blue bead from the bowl of 1,000 beads is 250 in 1,000 or 0.25.

One could also express the two proportions as percentages, namely, .1% and 25%, respectively. In statistics, the most common way of expressing probabilities is as a decimal proportion.

Multiplication Rule

From the previous example of the 250 blue, 250 red, and 500 while beads in a bowl, it was observed that the probability of drawing a blue bead on a single draw was 1 in 4 or 0.25, since only one-fourth of the beads are favorable to this outcome. The probability of drawing a red bead is, likewise, 1 in 4 or 0.25. But, the probability of drawing a white bead is 1 in 2 since one-half of the beads are favorable to this outcome.

Suppose two draws are made; the first bead is replaced after being drawn. What is the probability that the first bead will be blue and the second bead will be white? The probability of event B (blue) followed by event W (white) is the product of the two probabilities:

$$(1/4) \times (1/2) \qquad = \qquad 1/8$$

or

$$(0.25) \times (0.50) \qquad = \qquad 0.125$$

Since the probability of drawing a white bead in no way depends upon the outcome of the first draw, event B and W are expressed as *independent*. *If two or more events are independent, the probability that they will all occur is the product of their separate probabilities.* This statement of the relationships of probabilities is referred to as the multiplication rule. Notice that here each bead was replaced after each draw so that the probabilities remain the same on each successive draw, regardless of what happened on the previous draw. This is also an example of random sampling with replacement.

Addition Rule

What is the probability that on a single draw the bead will be either a blue or a white bead? *The probability that one of a number of mutually exclusive events(those that cannot occur at the same time) will occur is the sum of the probabilities that the separate events will occur.* This statement of relationships and probabilities is the rule of addition. Applying this rule to the sample, the probability of either event B or event W occurring would be:

$$\frac{1}{4} + \frac{1}{2} \qquad = \qquad \frac{3}{4}$$

or

$$0.25 + 0.50 \qquad = \qquad 0.75$$

Conditional Probability

Rather than replace the bead after each draw, suppose the sampling procedure is modified by not replacing the drawn bead. (This is an example of random sampling without replacement.) On the first draw, the probabilities of selecting a blue, red, or white bead remain the same as before. But the probabilities on the second draw have changed slightly because there is one less bead of the same color. On the third draw the probabilities are different from either the first or the second draw. The probabilities on each successive draw are affected by the prior events that have taken place. This relationship is referred to as "conditional probability," sometimes called "dependent probability." When the probability of an event is changed by the occurrence or nonoccurrence of another event, the two events are not independent. *If two events are not independent, the probability that both events will occur is the product of the probability of the first event and the probability of the second, if the first has occurred.*

If we make three selections from the bowl of beads without replacement, what is the probability that the first three will be blue, red, and white? The probability of drawing a blue bead on the first draw is 250/100 or 0.25. The probability of drawing a red bead on the second draw would be 250/999, or 0.2503, since there is one less bead in the bowl. The probability of drawing a white bead on the third draw would be 500/998, or 0.5010 since there are two less beads in the bowl. The conditional probability of drawing a white bead if one blue and one red have already been drawn would be 0.5010. The probability of selecting blue, red, and white, on the first three draws, without replacement, is:

$$(0.250)(0.2503)(0.5010) = \qquad 0.0314$$

In statistical notations, when a confidence level of 0.95 is specified, this is actually a probability of 0.95 or 95 in 100 or 19 in 20 chances that a certain event will occur. Similarly, when the 0.90 level of confidence is specified, this is actually a probability of 0.90 or that a certain event should happen 90 times in 100 (9 in 10 chances).

APPENDIX C

NORMAL DISTRIBUTION TABLES

Table C.1 (on the next page) is considered a double-entry table and requires locating the proper row and column before reading an entry in the body of the table. The entries in the body of the table represent the proportion of the total area under a normal curve (distribution) lying between the mean and the specific Z-score. For example, the area corresponding to a Z-score of 1.35 can be found by locating the row labeled 1.3 and the column labeled .05 and is seen to be .41149. The area (proportion) found in the body of the table and the corresponding Z-score are illustrated in the normal distribution (curve) figure that follows. All other proportions can be read in the same way.

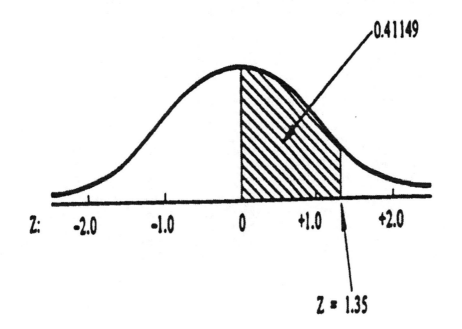

Due to the symmetry of the normal distribution, the tabular values also apply to standard scores in the negative direction.

TABLE C.1 PROPORTIONS OF AREAS UNDER THE NORMAL CURVE BETWEEN THE MEAN AND Z-SCORES FROM 0.00 TO 3.09

Z	.00	.01	.02	.03	.04	.05	.06	.07	.08	.09
0.0	.00000	.00399	.00798	.01197	.01595	.01994	.02392	.02790	.03188	.03586
0.1	.03983	.04380	.04776	.05172	.05567	.05962	.06356	.06749	.07142	.07535
0.2	.07926	.08317	.08706	.09095	.09483	.09871	.10257	.10642	.11026	.11409
0.3	.11791	.12172	.12552	.12930	.13307	.13683	.14058	.14431	.14803	.15173
0.4	.15542	.15910	.16276	.16640	.17003	.17364	.17724	.18082	.18439	.18793
0.5	.19146	.19497	.19847	.20194	.20540	.20884	.21226	.21566	.21904	.22240
0.6	.22575	.22907	.23237	.23565	.23891	.24215	.24537	.24857	.25175	.25490
0.7	.25804	.26115	.26424	.26730	.27035	.27337	.27637	.27935	.28230	.28524
0.8	.28814	.29103	.29389	.29673	.29955	.30234	.30511	.30785	.31057	.31327
0.9	.31594	.31859	.32121	.32381	.32639	.32894	.33147	.33398	.33646	.33891
1.0	.34134	.34375	.34614	.34850	.35083	.35314	.35543	.35769	.35993	.36214
1.1	.36433	.36650	.36864	.37076	.37286	.37493	.37698	.37900	.38100	.38298
1.2	.38493	.38686	.38877	.39065	.39251	.39435	.39617	.39796	.39973	.40147
1.3	.40320	.40490	.40658	.40824	.40988	.41149	.41309	.41466	.41621	.41774
	.41924	.42073	.42220	.42364	.42507	.42647	.42786	.42922	.43056	.43189
1.5	.43319	.43448	.43574	.43699	.43822	.43943	.44062	.44179	.44295	.44408
1.6	.44520	.44630	.44738	.44845	.44950	.45053	.45154	.45254	.45352	.45449
1.7	.45543	.45637	.45728	.45818	.45907	.45994	.46080	.46164	.46246	.46327
1.8	.46407	.46485	.46562	.46638	.46712	.46784	.46856	.46926	.46995	.47062
1.9	.47128	.47193	.47257	.47320	.47381	.47441	.47500	.47558	.47615	.47670
2.0	.47725	.47778	.47831	.47882	.47932	.47982	.48030	.48077	.48124	.48169
2.1	.48214	.48257	.48300	.48341	.48382	.48422	.48461	.48500	.48537	.48574
2.2	.48610	.48645	.48679	.48713	.48745	.48778	.48809	.48840	.48870	.48899
2.3	.48928	.48956	.48983	.49010	.49036	.49061	.49086	.49111	.49134	.49158
2.4	.49180	.49202	.49224	.49245	.49266	.49286	.49305	.49324	.49343	.49361
2.5	.49379	.49396	.49413	.49430	.49446	.49461	.49477	.49492	.49506	.49520
2.6	.49534	.49547	.49560	.49573	.49585	.49598	.49609	.49621	.49632	.49643
2.7	.49653	.49664	.49674	.49683	.49693	.49702	.49711	.49720	.49728	.49736
2.8	.49745	.49752	.49760	.49767	.49774	.49781	.49788	.49795	.49801	.49807
2.9	.49813	.49819	.49825	.49831	.49836	.49841	.49846	.49851	.49856	.49861
3.0	.49865	.49869	.49874	.49878	.49882	.49886	.49889	.49893	.49897	.49900

TABLE C.2 SELECTED Z-SCORES ASSOCIATED WITH PROPORTIONS OF
AREAS UNDER THE NORMAL CURVE FOR PROPORTIONS FROM .05 TO .499

Z-Score	Proportion of Area from Mean to Z-Score
.126	.05
.253	.10
.385	.15
.524	.20
.6745	.25
.842	**.30**
1.036	.35
1.282	.40
1.645	.45
1.960	.475
2.326	.49
2.576	.495
3.09	.499

In Table C.2, the Z-scores corresponding to specific proportions can be determined without unnecessary interpolation in Table C.1. The proportion of the total area under the normal curve from the mean to the given Z-score is found in the right hand column of the table and the associated Z-score on the same row in the first column of the table. If it is desired to identify the appropriate Z-score associated with .30 of the area under the normal curve, from Table C.2 in the boxed and shaded row this Z-score can be seen to be .842 and is also indicated in the normal curve below.

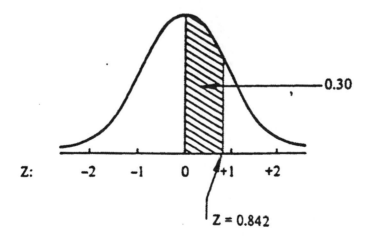

APPENDIX D

GLOSSARY

The following letter from a student, obviously written tongue in cheek, suggests a clear reason why a Glossary is extremely important in any subject, particularly one, such as statistics, in which words and phrases may have meanings totally different from what one might encounter elsewhere.

October 7, 1992

Dear Dr. McCALL,

As a cop I understand words like deviant, bisexual, paramedics and hypodermic, but I had some trouble with deviation, bivariate, parameters and hypothesis.

To me, a sample is something that goes in a urine bottle, and the analysis unit is where you have the samples analyzed. The range is where we go to shoot, and mean is what people accuse us of being. Value is what the stolen item was worth, and a normal distribution means you do your fair share of the work. Dispersion is what you do when the crowd gets out of control. The median is in the center of the road, and classification is how we cluster our jail population.

Relative to homogeneity, frequency, graphic display, positional, heterogeneity, etc. I choose to leave these to the average deviation of ones own factor analysis.

The point of all this is that I found your glossary to be somewhat limited, so I added a few words to round out the field. Once I got a grasp of the terminology, the rest was easy.

Since the work is already done, I thought you might want to share this with other students to update the glossary. Hypothetically, my factors are formatted in a precision manner, but you may want to do a discriminant analysis, or at least a random sampling.

Respectfully,

Arthur F. Ames

GLOSSARY

PLEASE NOTE THAT TERMS IN GLOSSARY MAY BE EITHER SINGULAR OR PLURAL.

Abscissa: The X-axis or the horizontal axis in a scatter plot. The axis which provides the values for the independent variable.

Analysis of covariance (ANCOVA): a statistical methodology used in inference to test the significance of differences among averages, after making an adjustment for the possible linear effect of one or more independent variables.

Analysis of variance (ANOVA): a statistical methodology used in inference to test the significance of differences among averages.

Analysis Unit (AU): the object or entity on which an observation or measurement is to be made for attributes or variables. For example, if a study is to be conducted on an educational issue, the analysis unit might be a student, a teacher, a registered voter, a school, or even a school district (or system).

ANCOVA: Please see *Analysis of covariance.*

ANOVA: Please see *Analysis of Variance.*

Arithmetic Mean: the simple average of all the numerical values associated with a single variable. Sometimes referred to as the simple average. (NOTE: characteristic **must** be a variable, not an attribute)

Association Measures: Measures, which are used to examine the relationship between two or more characteristics. Please see *correlation and regression.*

Attribute: a characteristic of an analysis unit that is naturally described by a name or a phrase. For example, if a teacher is the analysis unit, then an attribute might be SEX, clearly described as male or female. Also, in a survey where an opinion item is presented, the attribute might be a RESPONSE, such as strongly agree, moderately agree, no opinion, moderately disagree, strongly disagree.

AU: Please see *Analysis unit.*

Average Deviation: the average amount by which the numerical values of a variable differ (in absolute value) from some central point, usually the arithmetic mean. (See also the *Standard deviation*.)

Bi-modal: a situation in which the characteristic being considered has two modes; one in which two categories or classes have the frequency of occurrence most heavily concentrated.

Binomial: an attribute that has two names, or descriptors, such as SEX (male versus female). The same as dichotomous, meaning two alternatives.

Biserial correlation: an examination of two characteristics, one of which is a variable and the other a binomial.

Bivariate: an analysis in which there are two variables involved, one of which is usually referred to as the independent variable and the other as the dependent variable.

Categories or classes: groupings of the data. For attributes, the specific named classes, such as male and female; for variables, groupings for purposes of analysis, such as reporting AGES of AUs in intervals of 10 years.

Cell: a position in a contingency table which contains information on the frequency and percentages associated with the given column and row.

Cell frequency: the number of observations in a cross-tabulation associated with the intersection of a row and a column. For example, the number of males of a given ethnic background in the sample.

Central tendency: a summary measure that tends to indicate how or where the data for a given characteristic are concentrated. Most frequent measures are the arithmetic mean, median, and mode.

Characteristic: any descriptor that can be used to differentiate between one analysis unit and another analysis unit. Characteristics may be either attributes or variables. For example, if the analysis unit is a parent, then an attribute might be SEX, described as male or female, while a variable might be AGE, described by some numerical value.

Classification: see *Categories or classes*.

Clusters: natural groupings of analysis units (e.g., students in schools, church congregations, or nurses in hospitals.).

Coefficient of determination: the proportion of the variation (variability, differences) in the dependent variable (Y) explained by differences in the independent variable(s) (x).

Coefficient of X: see *Slope of the line*.

Collapsing: A practice of combining adjacent cells in a contingency table to eliminate cells with less than 5 observations.

Confidence level: the probability associated with confidence limits, usually 90%, 95%, or 99% in educational research.

Confidence limits: limits, based upon sample data, within which it is highly likely (referred to as the confidence level) that a population parameter (such as the arithmetic mean or a proportion) lies. These limits increase in size as the required confidence increases and as the acceptable error gets larger. These limits also decrease as the sample size increases.

Contingency coefficient: a measure of the extent of dependence existing in a two-way table. This measure is associated with a procedure referred to as chi-square.

Contingency table: Please see *Cross-tabs*.

Continuous variable: a characteristic that can assume, theoretically, an unlimited number of values. For example, the variable WEIGHT can be recorded to any number of decimal places, constrained only by the accuracy of the measuring instrument. Other examples would be AGE, HEIGHT, and TEMPERATURE.

Correlation: a concept in which relationships between two or more variables are studied. Existence of a significant correlation does not necessarily imply cause and effect.

Correlation coefficient: a measure of the linear relationship between two variables. It ranges from−1 to +1.

Covariate: In analyzing possible differences among averages, one might consider whether one or more independent variables, referred to as covariates, explain some of the differences in the dependent, or response variable.

Cross tabs or cross-tabulations: statistical tables in which the data associated with a group of analysis units are classified by at least two attributes or groupings of variables. For example, the distribution of ATTI-

TUDES (one attribute) for male and female respondents (a second attribute, SEX) in a survey. Cross tabs usually indicate the frequency for each category as well as appropriate percentages or proportions.

Cumulative frequency distribution: similar to a frequency distribution except for each interval the cumulative number of AUs less than each interval are indicated. Applies to variables only.

Cumulative percentage distribution: similar to a percentage distribution except for each interval the cumulative percentage of AUs less than each interval is indicated. Applies to variables only.

Database: a file which includes all characteristics of interest (both attributes and variables) for the AUs in a given sample or population. The information for a given AU in this database is usually referred to as a record.

Dependent variable(s): those variables in a sample or population that may be dependent upon other variables. For example, COLLEGE FRESHMAN GRADE POINT AVERAGES (the dependent variable) may be dependent upon SCHOLASTIC APTITUDE TEST SCORES.

Descriptive statistics: that segment of the subject called statistics in which data are used to describe a given sample or population. (See *inferential statistics*.)

Dichotomous: for an attribute, meaning there are only two alternatives. For example, male versus female, yes versus no, or true versus false.

Discriminant Analysis: a statistical procedure for identifying which, among a set of characteristics associated with an analysis unit, can serve to assign each analysis unit to one of two or more distinct categories or classifications. For example, a process which might identify which characteristics could serve to differentiate between individuals who are likely to succeed in college and those who are not likely to succeed in college.

Discrete variable: a variable that can assume only integral values, such as NUMBER OF CHILDREN IN A CLASSROOM or TEST SCORES.

Dispersion (or variation): the tendency for a variable to assume more than a single value. Large dispersion of a variable suggests a heterogeneous group whereas a small dispersion suggests a more homogeneous group.

Disk operating system (DOS): a specific operating system that provides the personal computer with the ability to handle and manipulate software. Acts somewhat like a policeman in directing data traffic. Examples of such operating systems might be Windows, UNIX and the MAC OS.

Distribution free: Please see *non-parametric methods*.

Distributions: for either attributes or variables, the distribution identifies the number and/or percentage of AUs contained in each category or classification. For example, 30% responded yes and 70% responded no to a question.

DOS: see *Disk Operating System*.

Error: in discussing estimates of population parameters, the error associated with the estimate indicates how accurate or how close the estimate is to the parameter. For example, in describing the percentage of respondents to a survey who support an issue, one might state that the estimate has an error of±.05. See also *Precision*.

Estimation: The process in statistical inference in which a sample statistic (such as the sample arithmetic mean or proportion) is used as an estimate of the corresponding population parameter.

Experimental design: a research methodology in which the analysis units are assigned randomly to various factors or main effects and then an intervention or interventions occur, with the study examining any possible differences in response or outcome variables. Usually involves some form of the analysis of variance or covariance..

Factor: one of several characteristics by which analysis units may be classified in an analysis of variance (See ***ANOVA***) or analysis of covariance (See ***ANCOVA***). See also ***Main effect***.

Factor Analysis: any of several complex statistical procedures for analyzing the interrelationships among a set of characteristics for the purpose of identifying the factors, preferably few in number, that cause these interrelationships. For example, if a large battery of tests is given to individuals for purposes of predicting, say, achievement, it is conceivable that this large set of tests (say 25) might, in fact, be measuring only five underlying constructs or concepts. Factor analysis examines the larger set of 25 variables to determine whether there might be interrelationships among these 25 that could be explained by five underlying factors? or constructs. Factor analysis is widely used in efforts to understand the organization of intelligence, personality, and also to assess whether a given instrument (e.g., a test or an opinion questionnaire) addresses the specific set of constructs for which the instrument was designed.

First quartile: That single positional measure corresponding to a value of a variable such that 25% of the observations in the distribution are less than the value of the variable. Conversely, 75% are greater than this first quartile point.

Frequency: an indication of the number of times a specific attribute or value for a variable occurs (e.g., 45 males and 72 females in a study; the 45 and 72 represent the frequencies).

Frequency distribution: an indication of the number of times specific attribute alternatives (say number of males and females) or intervals of values for variables (say ranges of INCOME) occur.

Graphic displays: visual presentations for a set of data. More commonly used graphics are bar charts, pie diagrams, histograms, line diagrams, scattergrams and Pareto diagrams.

Heterogeneity: the tendency for a set of data to exhibit large dispersion (individual values are far apart).

Homogeneity: the tendency for a set of data to exhibit small dispersion (individual values are close together).

Hypothesis: an unproved theory, proposition, or guess (hopefully educated). (See ***Null hypothesis***).

Hypothesis testing: The process in statistical inference in which a sample statistic, or several sample statistics (such as the sample arithmetic mean or proportion), are used to test hypotheses about the parameter, or parameters, of the population(s) from which the sample(s) were selected.

Independent Variable: that variable or variables, usually referred to by the letter X, in a regression analysis which are used to predict values for the dependent variable.

Inference: Please see ***inferential statistics***.

Inferential statistics: that segment of the subject called statistics in which data are used to make statements about a population based upon a sample or samples drawn from that population. (See ***Descriptive statistics***.)

Inferential techniques: Those statistical procedures that permit one to make statements about whether sample results are consistent or inconsistent with hypotheses regarding a population or populations.

Interaction: an effect in the analysis of variance which is observed when looking at two or more factors at the same time, as opposed to examining the response variable for each factor one at a time. For example, as

AGE increases among a group of graduate students, the scores of MALE students may change differently from the scores of FEMALE students.

Inter-quartile range: that range for a variable which has been ranked or ordered which contains the middle 50% of the observations in the sample or population. Frequently; referred to as the difference between the 75th percentile and the 25th percentile (See *percentiles*).

Interval: usually ranges of values in a frequency distribution; for example, grouping individuals in age intervals.

Least squares: The theoretical mathematical process used to estimate the regression equations from a set of sample data, such that the errors in prediction are minimized.

Level of confidence: See *Confidence level*.

Level of significance: represents the risk one is willing to take in rejecting a null hypothesis when it is true. Usually taken, as .10, .05, or .01 in educational research.

Likert scale: A scale of measurement, usually used with attributes which can be ordered, and which permits numerical values to be assigned to the specific attribute categories. For example, if one is conducting an opinion survey, a characteristic of interest might be how one feels about specific issues. The responses might be *strongly favor, favor, neither favor nor oppose, oppose*, and *strongly oppose*. This scale is referred to as a Likert scale and usually has numerical values assigned to the five word categories, such as *1, 2, 3, 4*, and *5*, respectively. A second characteristic of a Likert scale is that, for items which address the same concept, the numerical Likert values can be added and averaged to obtain an average score, or Likert value, for the set of like items.

Linear comparisons: See *Linear contrasts*.

Linear contrasts: Comparisons made between two or more arithmetic means as part of a process to determine which means are statistically different from each other. Please see *linear comparisons*.

Main effect: In analyzing possible differences among arithmetic means, a main effect is a way in which an analysis unit has been classified for the study. For example, one may wish to modify a curriculum in a given program. A classical approach might be considered, as well as two new more technological approaches. The main effect here would be curriculum type. One might also consider possible differences among male and female students in this project. SEX now becomes an additional main effect. (See also *Factor*.)

Marginal frequencies: in a cross-tabulation, the total frequencies associated with a given row or a given column.

Marginal percentages: in a cross-tabulation, the percentage each row or column total is of the total sample size.

Matrix: A mathematical array of numerical values. Please see *Cross-tabs* or *cross-tabulations*.

Mean: the simple average of the set of observations. Applies to variables only.

Measures of central tendency: see *Central tendency*.

Measures of dispersion: summary measures that enable the researcher to describe the variability or dispersion in a sample or a population. Examples are the range, inter-quartile range, average deviation, and standard deviation.

Measures of variation: see *Measures of dispersion*.

Median: the middle value, or central point, for a variable that has been ranked or ordered.

Mode: that value for a variable or that category for an attribute that occurs most often. The mode, or modal value, may not exist or there may be several modes (See *Bi-modal*).

Multinomial distribution: an attribute that has more than two categories or classes. For example, ETHNIC-ITY may be described by four or five separate identifiers. The distribution of ethnicity in a sample or population is referred to as a multinomial distribution.

Non-parametric methods: Statistical methodologies used in inference to test various hypotheses. Assumptions about the populations are less rigorous than for parametric methods.

Normal Distribution: the familiar bell-shaped curve in which the mean, median, and mode are equal. This distribution possesses certain properties that are extremely important in the development of statistical inference.

Null hypothesis: generally an hypothesis stating there is no difference or no relationship among the categories being studied. For example, one might test the hypothesis that there is no difference in average achievement among a group of students who are exposed to three different methods of instruction.

Observation or observations: the set of characteristics associated with a single analysis unit.

One-way table: A table that gives the frequency distribution (possibly percentages) for a single characteristic, such as AGE or SEX.

Ordinate: The Y-axis or the vertical axis in a scatter plot. The axis which provides the values for the dependent variable.

Outcome: See *Response*.

P value: That calculated value, associated with testing hypotheses, indicating the probability of obtaining the specific sample results or less likely results under the assumption that the null hypothesis is true.

Parameter: a constant or fixed value of a summary or descriptive measure in a population, fixed at any point in time. For example, the average AGE of a group of employees of a given company or me proportion of analysis units who support a given political issue. A parameter is to a population as a statistic is to a sample.

Parametric analysis: Please see *parametric methods*.

Parametric methods: statistical methodologies used in inference to test various hypotheses. Examples would be the analysis of variance, analysis of covariance or multiple regression. Sets more rigorous requirements on assumptions about the populations from which the samples have been selected.

P.C.: In the context of this manual, a P.C. is a personal computer of any type , whether IBM, Mac, or such others as Dell, Compaq, or Gateway.

Pearson's product-moment correlation coefficient: see *Correlation coefficient*.

Percentage distribution: usually a table that identifies the percentage of AUs in specific intervals or in specific groups, such as males and females. (see frequency distribution)

Percentile: a positional score, associated with a specific value of a variable, which identifies the percentage (or proportion) of values of the variable less than the specific value of the variable.

Personal Computer (P. C.): usually a desktop or portable computer characterized by a small size. Some more common P.C.s are IBM, Compaq, Macintosh, Gateway and Dell.

Phi coefficient: a measure of the extent of dependence between two truly dichotomous characteristics.

Point Biserial coefficient: a measure of the extent of dependence between two dichotomous characteristics when one of the characteristics may have been forced into dichotomous classification, such as two age groupings.

Population: the entire group or set of analysis units under consideration in a study or project. Also referred to as "universe."

Positional measure: a positional measure indicates the relative position of an observation for a variable within a specific sample or population. Examples of positional measures are percentiles and standard scores.

Precision: in discussing estimates of population parameters, the precision of the estimate indicates how accurate or how close the estimate is to the parameter being estimated. For example, in describing the percentage of respondents to a survey who support an issue, one might state that the estimate has a precision of±.05. See also *Error*.

Probability: the relative frequency or likelihood that a specific observation or range of values might occur. For example, in tossing an unbiased coin the probability that a head will occur is 0.50.

Probability value: Please see *P-value*.

Random Sampling: a method for selecting analysis units from a population in such a manner that the probability of selecting each analysis unit is known. This probability of selection is usually taken as being equal for all analysis units, but is not necessarily so (e.g., when stratified sampling is done disproportionately).

Random sampling with replacement: a random sampling process, usually associated with small populations, in which an AU, after being selected is returned to the sampling frame and is available for selection again.

Random sampling without replacement: a random sampling process in which an AU, after being selected, is not eligible to be selected a second time, as in *Sampling with replacement*.

Range: the distance between the largest and the smallest value for a variable. For example the range of TEST SCORES might be from 65 to 95, or 30 units.

Record: a listing of all the characteristics associated with an analysis unit. In a spreadsheet a record is usually a row of data.

Regression: a statistical methodology in which one dependent variable is studied in terms of its possible relationship, or predictability, from one or more independent variables. Usually results in a regression, or predicting, equation.

Regression line: the line that describes the mathematical relationship between a dependent variable and one or more independent variables. Please see *Least squares*.

Relational measures: summary measures, such as the correlation coefficient, which identify the extent of a possible relationship among two or more characteristics.

Relative measures: summary measures that position an observation within a group, such as the standard score or percentile. Please see also *positional measures*.

Research hypothesis: A hypothesis usually based upon previous research. For example, one might hypothesize that the use of personal computers as a tool in teaching writing at the elementary school level would improved achievement scores over students who were exposed to other methods of teaching writing.

Research Question: A question, usually generated by a problem ,issue or dilemma, in which data are needed to provide information to assess the question. In most cases, a research question differences from a research hypothesis in that prior research exists from which a research hypothesis may have been generated.

Response: in the analysis of variance or covariance, the response variable is usually the dependent variable of interest in the research. For example, in studying various approaches to accomplishing a specific task, the response variable might be *time to complete the task.* Please see **Outcome**.

Risk: See *Level of significance.*

Sample: a group or set of analysis units selected from a larger set (referred to as the population or universe). For example. a sample of 200 registered voters taken from a listing of all registered voters. NOTE: the word sample does not necessarily connote "goodness" or "representativeness."

Scatter plot: a graph in which observations on two variables are plotted on an X,Y-axis. For example, a plot of aptitude scores (x) versus achievement scores (Y).

Sampling Frame: the listing of all analysis units of interest in a project or study.

Slope of the line: in the bivariate situation the slope of the line indicates the expected change in the dependent variable (Y) for a unit change in the independent variable (x).

Spearman 's rho (ρ): similar to the Pearson's product-moment correlation coefficient but used when examining the extent of a possible relationship between two characteristics which have been ranked.

Standard deviation: a measure of the variability about the arithmetic mean of a set of observations.

Standard error of the mean: Used to describe the standard deviation of the distribution of all possible sample means from a given population.

Standard Score: any one of a number of derived statistics which identify the position of a given value of a variable in terms of its relationship to the arithmetic mean of the group of observations. The most familiar is the Z Score that indicates the number of standard deviations an observation is above or below the average (mean) for the sample or population.

Statistic: a summary or descriptive measure in a sample, subject to variability from sample to sample drawn from the same population. For example, the average income of a sample of faculty drawn from a given university or the proportion of a sample of registered voters who support a given issue. A statistic is to a sample as a parameter is to a population.

Statistical hypothesis: usually that hypothesis which is being tested, the rejection of which might support the researcher's research hypothesis.

Statistical inference: that statistical methodology in which information contained in a sample or samples is generalized to the population from which the sample(s) has been selected. There are two major categories of inference: estimation and hypothesis testing.

Statistics: A discipline (much like mathematics and engineering are disciplines) which calls for planning and the collection, tabulation, analysis, interpretation and presentation of information.

Strata: groupings of an analysis unit, usually selected to be certain that a particular characteristic is in the sample or to allow for sample selection when no single sampling frame of AUs exists. We stratify by region of the country to assure representation from every region; we stratify by ethnic groups to assure representation from all ethnic groups in our sample.

Survey sampling: a research methodology in which data are collected by using a survey, such as by mail, telephone, or in person. This methodology is different from experimental design where the AUs are randomly assigned to factors and then an intervention occurs and responses observed.

Systematic Sampling with a Random Start: a method of selecting a sample by taking analysis units at fixed intervals within the sampling frame. The process calls for identifying the sampling interval (say I), the population size (say N), and then randomly selecting the starting point for the sampling within the first N/I analysis units in the population. NOTE: this process requires that the analysis units be arranged in some order within the sampling frame.

Tests of significance: those tests, such as chi-square and the analysis of variance, which are used to test specific hypotheses.

Tetrachoric correlation coefficient: a measure of association when both variables have been compressed into a dichotomous form and the underlying distribution for both variables is assumed to be normal.

Third quartile: That single positional measure corresponding to a value of a variable such that 75% of the observations in the distribution are less than the value of the variable. Conversely, 25% are greater than this third quartile point.

Two-Way distribution: a table which classifies the observations by two characteristics at the same time; for example, identifying the distribution of respondents to a political survey by their PARTY and their ETHNICITY. Please see also *Matrix* and *Cross-tabulations*.

Type I error: a rejection of the null hypothesis when it should not have been rejected.

Type II error: a non-rejection of the null hypothesis when it should have been rejected.

Universe: the entire group or set of analysis units under consideration in a study or project. Also referred to as "population."

Value label files: these are files that identify which names are associated with which numbers assigned to attributes in a database. For example, the value label file for the attribute SEX, might indicate that a male = 1 and a female = 2 in the database.

Variable: a characteristic of an analysis unit that is naturally described by some numerical value. For example, if the analysis unit is a STUDENT, then a variable might be the AGE of the student, which is naturally described by a numerical value.

Variance: this is the square of the standard deviation.

Y-intercept: in a regression analysis, the value for the Y variable when all of the independent variables are set equal to 0.

Z-Score: a standard score in which the original value of a variable is expressed as the number of standard deviations the original value is from the arithmetic mean of the set of observations. A Z score may be either positive or negative, depending upon whether the original score is above or below the average of the group. Z scores are particularly important when making use of properties of the normal distribution.

APPENDIX E

2SCH4 DATABASE

This database consists of the following:

1. Analysis unit: a high school student
2. Sample: Analysis units (AUs) from three consecutive graduating classes.
3. Sample size: 224
4. Characteristics:
   - 4.1 Sex
   - 4.2 Ethnicity
   - 4.3 Number of times taking the SAT
   - 4.4 SAT Verbal
   - 4.5 SAT Math
   - 4.6 Number of honors level English courses taken
   - 4.7 Highest level of math taken
   - 4.8 High school grade point average (GPA)
   - 4.9 Year of graduation (three consecutive years)

Data for this database comes from a dissertation at Pepperdine University Graduate School of Education and Psychology. Data which follow are only a part of the specific database. Please note that column headings may be slightly offset due to insertion of the database from the original statistical software.

Row	Stu_ID	Sch_ID	SEX	Ethnic	No_Sat	SATVER	SATMath	HonEng	HighMath	GPA	GradYear
1	1	4	1	1	3	440	490	1.0	3	3.480	1
2	2	4	1	1	1	370	320	1.0	2	2.920	1
3	3	4	2	1	2	370	420	1.0	3	2.910	1
4	4	4	1	1	2	510	610	2.5	5	4.000	1
5	5	4	2	1	2	330	510	1.0	3	3.460	1
6	6	4	2	1	2	510	490	2.5	3	3.730	1
7	7	4	1	1	3	550	670	2.5	3	3.560	1
8	8	4	2	1	2	480	380	1.0	2	2.370	1
9	9	4	1	1	1	590	710	2.5	5	3.820	1
10	10	4	1	1	3	500	660	1.0	5	3.730	1
11	11	4	1	1	1	630	650	2.5	4	3.650	1
12	12	4	1	1	2	560	500	2.5	3	2.650	1
13	13	4	2	1	2	560	590	2.5	5	3.630	1
14	14	4	1	1	1	420	550	1.5	5	2.730	1
15	15	4	1	1	2	470	580	2.0	4	3.650	1
16	16	4	1	1	2	560	540	2.5	5	4.000	1
17	17	4	1	4	1	290	550	0.0	3	2.760	1
18	18	4	2	1	1	530	350	2.5	2	2.940	1
19	19	4	1	1	1	230	410	0.0	2	2.950	1
20	20	4	2	1	1	310	310	0.0	2	2.870	1

Row	Stu_ID	Sch_ID	SEX	Ethnic	No_Sat	SATVER	SATMath	HonEng	HighMath	GPA	GradYear
21	21	4	1	1	2	410	400	0.5	3	2.650	1
22	22	4	1	1	1	580	650	1.5	4	3.760	1
23	23	4	1	1	2	350	370	1.0	2	2.730	1
24	24	4	2	1	1	370	370	1.0	1	2.780	1
25	25	4	2	1	1	270	340	1.5	1	3.150	1
26	26	4	2	1	2	370	360	1.0	2	3.050	1
27	27	4	2	1	2	300	450	1.0	2	2.580	1
28	28	4	2	1	1	450	450	0.5	2	2.460	1
29	29	4	2	1	1	490	430	2.0	2	3.200	1
30	30	4	1	1	1	460	610	0.5	3	2.510	1
31	31	4	1	1	2	390	490	1.5	3	3.370	1
32	32	4	1	1	1	430	400	0.0	1	2.340	1
33	33	4	2	1	1	350	370	1.0	2	2.960	1
34	34	4	2	1	1	290	310	0.0	1	2.540	1
35	35	4	1	3	1	380	510	0.0	2	3.130	1
36	36	4	2	1	2	440	560	2.0	3	3.550	1
37	37	4	2	1	1	330	290	1.0	1	2.690	1
38	38	4	2	5	1	380	350	1.0	3	3.000	1
39	39	4	2	1	1	580	340	2.5	3	3.270	1
40	40	4	1	1	1	520	620	1.0	4	2.900	1
41	41	4	1	1	1	310	460	1.0	2	2.650	1
42	42	4	1	1	1	500	390	2.0	2	3.310	1
43	43	4	2	1	1	370	420	2.0	3	2.960	1
44	44	4	2	1	1	460	400	0.5	1	2.470	1
45	45	4	2	1	1	570	430	2.5	2	3.550	1
46	46	4	1	1	2	500	670	2.5	5	4.000	1
47	47	4	1	1	3	420	450	1.5	3	3.620	1
48	48	4	2	1	1	610	670	2.5	4	3.410	1
49	49	4	2	1	1	610	470	2.0	2	3.180	1
50	50	4	1	1	1	490	460	1.5	2	2.730	1
51	51	4	1	1	1	430	480	0.5	2	2.300	1
52	52	4	2	3	1	270	270	1.5	3	3.470	1
53	53	4	2	1	1	320	360	0.0	2	2.650	1
54	54	4	2	1	1	430	470	1.0	2	2.700	1
55	55	4	1	1	1	230	460	1.0	2	2.750	1
56	56	4	1	4	1	660	700	2.5	4	4.000	1
57	57	4	2	1	1	400	440	1.5	2	3.020	1
58	58	4	2	1	1	400	300	0.5	2	2.350	1
59	59	4	1	4	1	390	450	0.5	2	2.400	1
60	60	4	2	1	2	360	450	1.0	2	3.180	1
61	61	4	1	1	1	380	360	0.5	2	2.610	1
62	62	4	1	1	1	600	640	2.0	3	2.670	1
63	63	4	1	1	1	460	380	2.5	2	3.190	1
64	64	4	2	1	1	470	420	2.5	3	3.190	1
65	65	4	1	1	1	310	370	0.0	2	2.710	1

Row	Stu_ID	Sch_ID	SEX	Ethnic	No_Sat	SATVER	SATMath	HonEng	HighMath	GPA	GradYear
66	1	4	1	1	1	450	570	2.0	3	3.470	2
67	2	4	2	1	1	330	300	0.5	2	2.420	2
68	3	4	1	1	2	330	400	1.0	2	2.240	2
69	4	4	1	1	1	350	480	0.5	2	2.650	2
70	5	4	1	6	2	430	360	1.0	4	2.930	2
71	6	4	1	4	1	340	600	0.0	3	2.350	2
72	7	4	2	1	2	430	460	1.0	3	2.810	2
73	8	4	2	1	1	500	400	1.0	3	2.990	2
74	9	4	1	1	3	470	590	3.0	5	3.750	2
75	10	4	1	3	2	550	640	1.0	5	3.310	2
76	11	4	2	1	1	390	400	1.0	1	2.350	2
77	12	4	1	6	2	480	440	1.0	2	1.740	2
78	13	4	2	1	1	420	400	0.5	3	2.090	2
79	14	4	2	1	2	470	580	1.0	5	2.770	2
80	15	4	1	1	2	460	390	1.0	2	2.770	2
81	16	4	2	1	2	370	440	3.0	2	2.350	2

Descriptive Statistics

Summary Section of SATVERB

Count	Mean	Standard Deviation	Standard Error	Minimum	Maximum	Range
224	426.5179	101.1478	6.758219	220	680	460

Counts Section of SATVERB

Rows	Sum of Frequencies	Missing Values	Distinct Values	Sum	Total Sum Squares	Adjusted Sum Squares
224	224	0	45	95540	4.3031E+07	2281484

Means Section of SATVERB

Parameter	Mean	Median	Geometric Mean	Harmonic Mean	Sum	Mode
Value	426.5179	430	414.2791	401.7513	95540	500
Std Error	6.758219				1513.841	
95% LCL	413.272	400			92572.93	
95% UCL	439.7637	440			98507.07	
T-Value	63.1110					
Prob Level	0.000000					
Count	224		224	224		14

Variation Section of SATVERB

Parameter	Variance	Standard Deviation	Unbiased Std Dev	Std Error of Mean	Interquartile Range	Range
Value	10230.87	101.1478	101.2612	6.758219	150	460
Std Error	832.0899	5.816999		0.3886646		
95% LCL	8568.874	92.56821		6.184974		
95% UCL	12430.87	111.4938		7.449495		

Skewness and Kurtosis Section of SATVERB

Parameter	Skewness	Kurtosis	Fisher's g1	Fisher's g2	Coefficient of Variation	Coefficient of Dispersion
Value	0.1950947	2.481711	0.1964124	−0.5027754	0.2371478	0.1920681
Std Error	0.106457	0.1556874			9.770826E–03	

Mean-Deviation Section of SATVERB

Parameter	|X-Mean|	|X-Median|	(X-Mean)^2	(X-Mean)^3	(X-Mean)^4
Average	82.62038	82.58929	10185.2	200539.4	2.574482E+08
Std Error	4.072796		828.3752	114380.3	3.743054E+07

Quartile Section of SATVERB

Parameter	10th Percentile	25th Percentile	50th Percentile	75th Percentile	90th Percentile
Value	290	350	430	500	560
95% LCL	280	330	400	480	550
95% UCL	310	370	440	510	590

Percentile Section of SATVERB

Percentile	Value	95% LCL	95% UCL	Exact Conf. Level
99	667.5			
95	607.5	580	630	95.1796
90	560	550	590	95.6185
85	540	510	560	95.0988
80	510	500	540	95.5037
75	500	480	510	95.5119
70	480	460	500	95.9005
65	460	450	490	95.0431
60	450	430	470	95.2007
55	440	420	460	95.6103
50	430	400	440	95.4740
45	410	390	430	95.6103
40	390	370	420	95.1464

Percentile	Value	95% LCL	95% UCL	Exact Conf. Level
35	380	370	400	95.0431
30	370	350	380	95.1159
25	350	330	370	95.4682
20	330	310	350	95.5037
15	310	290	330	96.0958
10	290	280	310	95.6185
5	270	230	290	95.5023
1	230			

Percentile Formula: Ave X(p[n+1])

Summary Section of SATMath

Count	Mean	Standard Deviation	Standard Error	Minimum	Maximum	Range
224	465.9821	119.3665	7.975509	250	760	510

Counts Section of SATMath

Rows	Sum of Frequencies	Missing Values	Distinct Values	Sum	Total Sum Squares	Adjusted Sum Squares
224	224	0	49	104380	5.18166E+07	3177384

Means Section of SATMath

Parameter	Mean	Median	Geometric Mean	Harmonic Mean	Sum	Mode
Value	465.9821	455	450.8409	435.9394	104380	
Std Error	7.975509				1786.514	
95% LCL	450.3504	430			100878.5	
95% UCL	481.6139	480			107881.5	
T-Value	58.4266					
Prob Level	0.000000					
Count	224		224	224		

Variation Section of SATMath

Parameter	Variance	Standard Deviation	Unbiased Std Dev	Std Error of Mean	Interquartile Range	Range
Value	14248.36	119.3665	119.5004	7.975509	190	510
Std Error	1067.521	6.323814		0.4225276		
95% LCL	11933.72	109.2416		7.299011		
95% UCL	17312.27	131.5761		8.791297		

Skewness and Kurtosis Section of SATMath

Parameter	Skewness	Kurtosis	Fisher's g1	Fisher's g2	Coefficient of Variation	Coefficient of Dispersion
Value	0.3468564	2.257394	0.3491992	−0.7321807	0.2561611	0.2158556
Std Error	9.941094E–02		0.1571227		9.233189E–03	

Mean-Deviation Section of SATMath

Parameter	|X-Mean|	|X-Median|	(X-Mean)^2	(X-Mean)^3	(X-Mean)^4
Average	98.74841	98.21429	14184.75	585979.3	4.542038E+08
Std Error	4.806387		1062.756	171020	5.706674E+07

Quartile Section of SATMath

Parameter	10th Percentile	25th Percentile	50th Percentile	75th Percentile	90th Percentile
Value	310	370	455	560	650
95% LCL	300	350	430	520	610
95% UCL	340	390	480	580	670

Percentile Section of SATMath

Percentile	Value	95% LCL	95% UCL	Exact Conf. Level
99	737.5			
95	670	660	710	95.1796
90	650	610	670	95.6185
85	610	580	640	95.0988
80	580	560	610	95.5037
Percentile	Value	95% LCL	95% UCL	Exact Conf. Level
75	560	520	580	95.5119
70	525	490	560	95.9005
65	500	480	530	95.0431
60	480	460	510	95.2007
55	470	450	490	95.6103
50	455	430	480	95.4740
45	440	410	460	95.6103
40	420	400	440	95.1464
35	400	390	420	95.0431
30	390	370	400	95.1159
25	370	350	390	95.4682
20	360	340	370	95.5037
15	340	310	360	96.0958
10	310	300	340	95.6185
5	290	270	300	95.5023
1	262.5			

Percentile Formula: Ave X(p[n+1])

Summary Section of GPA

Count	Mean	Standard Deviation	Standard Error	Minimum	Maximum	Range
224	2.966786	0.497964	3.327161E–02	1.33	4	2.67

Counts Section of GPA

Rows	Sum of Frequencies	Missing Values	Distinct Values	Sum	Total Sum Squares	Adjusted Sum Squares
224	224	0	122	664.56	2026.904	55.29689

Means Section of GPA

Parameter	Mean	Median	Geometric Mean	Harmonic Mean	Sum	Mode
Value	2.966786	2.92	2.923872	2.878907	664.56	2.65
Std Error	3.327161E–02				7.452842	
95% LCL	2.901575	2.82			649.9527	
95% UCL	3.031997	3			679.1673	
T-Value	89.1687					
Prob Level	0.000000					
Count	224		224	224		6

Variation Section of GPA

Parameter	Variance	Standard Deviation	Unbiased Std Dev	Std Error of Mean	Interquartile Range	Range
Value	0.2479681	0.497964	0.4985225	3.327161E–02	0.7149998	2.67
Std Error	2.171569E–02		3.083619E–02		2.06033E–03	
95% LCL	0.2076859	0.4557257		3.044945E–02		
95% UCL	0.3012901	0.548899		3.667486E–02		

Skewness and Kurtosis Section of GPA

Parameter	Skewness	Kurtosis	Fisher's g1	Fisher's g2	Coefficient of Variation	Coefficient of Dispersion
Value	5.318719E–02	2.717922	5.354643E–02	–0.261205	0.1678463	0.1381177
Std Error	0.159298	0.3276975			7.511505E–03	

Mean-Deviation Section of GPA

Parameter	|X-Mean|	|X-Median|	(X-Mean)^2	(X-Mean)^3	(X-Mean)^4
Average	0.4054879	0.4033036	0.2468611	6.52358E–03	0.1656313
Std Error	2.005092E–02		2.161874E–02	1.916807E–02	3.699996E–02

Quartile Section of GPA

Parameter	10th Percentile	25th Percentile	50th Percentile	75th Percentile	90th Percentile
Value	2.35	2.635	2.92	3.35	3.68
95% LCL	2.27	2.52	2.82	3.18	3.55
95% UCL	2.42	2.69	3	3.46	3.79

Percentile Section of GPA

Percentile	Value	95% LCL	95% UCL	Exact Conf. Level
99	4			
95	3.835	3.73	3.98	95.1796
90	3.68	3.55	3.79	95.6185
85	3.5425	3.46	3.65	95.0988
80	3.46	3.35	3.55	95.5037
75	3.35	3.18	3.46	95.5119
70	3.19	3.13	3.36	95.9005
65	3.1425	3.04	3.26	95.0431
60	3.07	2.95	3.15	95.2007
55	2.975	2.9	3.12	95.6103
50	2.92	2.82	3	95.4740
45	2.8625	2.76	2.94	95.6103
40	2.77	2.71	2.88	95.1464
35	2.73	2.67	2.81	95.0431
30	2.685	2.63	2.74	95.1159
25	2.635	2.52	2.69	95.4682
20	2.55	2.44	2.65	95.5037
15	2.44	2.35	2.55	96.0958
10	2.35	2.27	2.42	95.6185
5	2.2425	2.09	2.33	95.5023
1	1.77			

Percentile Formula: Ave X(p[n+1])

GPA versus SATVerbal

Regression Equation Section

Independent Variable	Regression Coefficient	Standard Error	T-Value (Ho: B = 0)	Prob Level	Decision (5%)	Power (5%)
Intercept	146.8789	36.32602	4.0434	0.000073	Reject Ho	0.980578
GPA	94.25654	12.07606	7.8052	0.000000	Reject Ho	1.000000
R-Squared	0.215331					

Regression Coefficient Section

Independent Variable	Regression Coefficient	Standard Error	Lower 95% C.L.	Upper 95% C.L.	Standardized Coefficient
Intercept	146.8789	36.32602	75.68124	218.0766	0.0000
GPA	94.25654	12.07606	70.5879	117.9252	0.4640
T-Critical	1.959964				

Analysis of Variance Section

Source	DF	Sum of Squares	Mean Square	F-Ratio	Prob Level	Power (5%)
Intercept	1	4.074952E+07		4.074952E+07		
Model	1	491273.8	491273.8	60.9218	0.000000	1.000000
Error	222	1790210	8064.01			
Total(Adjusted)	223	2281484	10230.87			

Root Mean Square Error	89.79983	R-Squared	0.2153
Mean of Dependent	426.5179	Adj R-Squared	0.2118
Coefficient of Variation	0.2105418	Press Value	1826209

CORRELATION MATRIX

	No_Sat	SATVERB	HonEng	GPA
No_Sat	1.000000	0.162819	0.180241	0.284636
SATVERB	0.162819	1.000000	0.536336	0.464038
HonEng	0.180241	0.536336	1.000000	0.536019
GPA	0.284636	0.464038	0.536019	1.000000

Cronbachs Alpha = 0.022627 Standardized Cronbachs Alpha = 0.692937

REGRESSION:SATVERB, No_SAT, HonEng, GPA

Regression Equation Section

Independent Variable (5%)	Regression Coefficient	Standard Error	T-Value (Ho: B = 0)	Prob	Decision Level	Power (5%)
Intercept	224.6647	36.23698	6.1999	0.000000	Reject Ho	0.999987
No_Sat	3.705119	9.995861	0.3707	0.711243	Accept Ho	0.065744
HonEng	40.24744	6.527962	6.1654	0.000000	Reject Ho	0.999985
GPA	49.17647	13.61374	3.6123	0.000376	Reject Ho	0.949132
R-Squared	0.331810					

Regression Coefficient Section

Independent Variable	Regression Coefficient	Standard Error	Lower 95% C.L.	Upper 95% C.L.	Standardized Coefficient
Intercept	224.6647	36.23698	153.6415	295.6878	0.0000
No_Sat	3.705119	9.995861	−15.88641	23.29665	0.0213
HonEng	40.24744	6.527962	27.45287	53.04201	0.4027
GPA	49.17647	13.61374	22.49404	75.85891	0.2421
T-Critical	1.959964				

Analysis of Variance Section

Source	DF	Sum of Squares	Mean Square	F-Ratio	Prob Level	Power (5%)
Intercept	1	4.074952E+07	4.074952E+07			
Model	3	757019.5	252339.8	36.4159	0.000000	0.999695
Error	220	1524465	6929.384			
Total(Adjusted)	223	2281484	10230.87			

Root Mean Square Error	83.24292	R-Squared	0.3318
Mean of Dependent	426.5179	Adj R-Squared	0.3227
Coefficient of Variation	0.1951687	Press Value	1580277
Sum |Press Residuals|	15659.16	Press R-Squared	0.3073

REGRESSION:SATVERB, HonEng, GPA

Regression Equation Section

Independent Variable	Regression Coefficient	Standard Error	T-Value (Ho: B = 0)	Prob Level	Decision (5%)	Power (5%)
Intercept	226.0991	35.95937	6.2876	0.000000	Reject Ho	0.999991
HonEng	40.33017	6.511401	6.1938	0.000000	Reject Ho	0.999987
GPA	50.31907	13.23425	3.8022	0.000186	Reject Ho	0.966048
R-Squared	0.331393					

Regression Coefficient Section

Independent Variable	Regression Coefficient	Standard Error	Lower 95% C.L.	Upper 95% C.L.	Standardized Coefficient
Intercept	226.0991	35.95937	155.62	296.5781	0.0000
HonEng	40.33017	6.511401	27.56806	53.09229	0.4035
GPA	50.31907	13.23425	24.38042	76.25772	0.2477
T-Critical	1.959964				

Analysis of Variance Section

Source	DF	Sum of Squares	Mean Square	F-Ratio	Prob Level	Power (5%)
Intercept	1	4.074952E+07	4.074952E+07			
Model	2	756067.4	378033.7	54.7689	0.000000	1.000000
Error	221	1525417	6902.337			
Total(Adjusted)	223	2281484	10230.87			

Root Mean Square Error	83.08031	R-Squared	0.3314
Mean of Dependent	426.5179	Adj R-Squared	0.3253
Coefficient of Variation	0.1947874	Press Value	1567745
Sum |Press Residuals|	15619.83	Press R-Squared	0.3128

REGRESSION:SATVERB, GPA

Regression Equation Section

Independent Variable	Regression Coefficient	Standard Error	T-Value (Ho: B = 0)	Prob Level	Decision (5%)	Power (5%)
Intercept	146.8789	36.32602	4.0434	0.000073	Reject Ho	0.980578
GPA	94.25654	12.07606	7.8052	0.000000	Reject Ho	1.000000
R-Squared	0.215331					

Regression Coefficient Section

Independent Variable	Regression Coefficient	Standard Error	Lower 95% C.L.	Upper 95% C.L.	Standardized Coefficient
Intercept	146.8789	36.32602	75.68124	218.0766	0.0000
GPA	94.25654	12.07606	70.5879	117.9252	0.4640
T-Critical	1.959964				

Analysis of Variance Section

Source	DF	Sum of Squares	Mean Square	F-Ratio	Prob Level	Power (5%)
Intercept	1	4.074952E+07		4.074952E+07		
Model	1	491273.8	491273.8	60.9218	0.000000	1.000000
Error	222	1790210	8064.01			
Total(Adjusted)	223	2281484	10230.87			

Root Mean Square Error	89.79983	R-Squared	0.2153
Mean of Dependent	426.5179	Adj R-Squared	0.2118
Coefficient of Variation	0.2105418	Press Value	1826209
Sum |Press Residuals|	16880.61	Press R-Squared	0.1996

ANOVA: SATVERB: SEX

Analysis of Variance Table

Source Term	DF	Sum of Squares	Mean Square	F-Ratio	Prob Level	Power (Alpha = 0.05)
A: SEX	1	11664.53	11664.53	1.14	0.286633	0.186249
S	222	2269820	10224.41			
Total (Adjusted)		223	2281484			
Total	224					

* Term significant at alpha = 0.05

Means and Standard Error Section

Term	Count	Mean	Standard Error
All	224	426.1954	
A: SEX			
1	117	433.4188	9.348162
2	107	418.972	9.775236

Plots Section

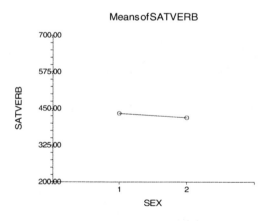

Means of SATVERB

ANOVA: SATMath: Graduation Year

Analysis of Variance Table

Source Term	DF	Sum of Squares	Mean Square	F-Ratio	Prob Level	Power (Alpha = 0.05)
A: GradYear	2	291023.8	145511.9	11.14	0.000025*	0.991531
S	221	2886360	13060.45			
Total (Adjusted)		223	3177384			
Total	224					

* Term significant at alpha = 0.05

Means and Standard Error Section

Term	Count	Mean	Standard Error
All	224	466.9179	
A: GradYear			
1	65	466.6154	14.17498
2	82	424.2683	12.62037
3	77	509.8701	13.02368

Plots Section

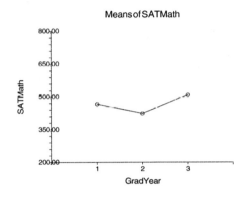

Fisher's LSD Multiple-Comparison Test
Response: SATMath
Term A: GradYear
Alpha = 0.050 Error Term = S(A) DF = 221 MSE = 13060.45 Critical Value = 1.959964

Group	Count	Mean	Different From Groups
2	82	424.2683	1, 3
1	65	466.6154	2, 3
3	77	509.8701	2, 1

ANOVA: SATMath, GradYear, Sex

Analysis of Variance Table

Source Term	DF	Sum of Squares	Mean Square	F-Ratio	Prob Level	Power (Alpha = 0.05)
A: GradYear	2	250384.5	125192.3	10.52	0.000043*	0.987043
B: SEX	1	269484.8	269484.8	22.65	0.000004*	0.996883
AB	2	39666.13	19833.07	1.67	0.191276	0.344769
S	218	2594190	11899.95			
Total (Adjusted)	223	3177384				
Total	224					

* Term significant at alpha = 0.05

Means and Standard Error Section

Term	Count	Mean	Standard Error
All	224	464.8272	
A: GradYear			
1	65	464.203	13.53057
2	82	425.2027	12.04663
3	77	505.0757	12.43161
B: SEX			
1	117	499.822	10.08509
2	107	429.8324	10.54583
AB: GradYear,SEX			
1,1	34	516.4706	18.70825
1,2	31	411.9355	19.59259
2,1	39	444.359	17.46788
2,2	43	406.0465	16.6356
3,1	44	538.6364	16.44547
3,2	33	471.5151	18.98959

Fisher's LSD Multiple-Comparison Test

Group	Count	Mean	Different From Groups
2	82	425.2027	1, 3
1	65	464.203	2, 3
3	77	505.0757	2, 1

Fisher's LSD Multiple-Comparison Test

Response: SATMath

Term AB: GradYear,SEX

Alpha = 0.050 Error Term = S(AB) DF = 218 MSE = 11899.95 Critical Value = 1.959964

Group	Count	Mean	Different From Groups
2,2	43	406.0465	(3,2), (1,1), (3,1)
1,2	31	411.9355	(3,2), (1,1), (3,1)
2,1	39	444.359	(1,1), (3,1)
3,2	33	471.5151	(2,2), (1,2), (3,1)
1,1	34	516.4706	(2,2), (1,2), (2,1)
3,1	44	538.6364	(2,2), (1,2), (2,1), (3,2)

ANOVA: SATMath,SEX, HighMath

Analysis of Variance Table

Source Term	DF	Sum of Squares	Mean Square	F-Ratio	Prob Level	Power (Alpha = 0.05)
A: SEX	1	13070.57	13070.57	2.09	0.149738	0.290409
B: HighMath	5	1213201	242640.2	38.80	0.000000*	1.000000
AB	5	16203.87	3240.775	0.52	0.762349	0.186179
S	212	1325788	6253.718			
Total (Adjusted)	223	3177384				
Total	224					

* Term significant at alpha = 0.05

Means and Standard Error Section

Term	Count	Mean	Standard Error
All	224	451.0027	
A: SEX			
1	117	464.0876	7.31099
2	107	437.9178	7.644996
B: HighMath			
0	5	290	35.36585
1	17	358.8333	19.17983

Term	Count	Mean	Standard Error
2	80	406.2822	8.841463
3	61	464.4318	10.12521
4	35	557.8497	13.36704
5	26	628.619	15.50895
AB: SEX,HighMath			
1,0	2	290	55.91832
1,1	2	385	55.91832
1,2	37	408.3784	13.00075
1,3	33	486.3636	13.76614
1,4	22	569.5455	16.86001
1,5	21	645.2381	17.25677
2,0	3	290	45.65712
2,1	15	332.6667	20.41848
2,2	43	404.186	12.05966
2,3	28	442.5	14.9448
2,4	13	546.1539	21.93297
2,5	5	612	35.36585

Plots Section

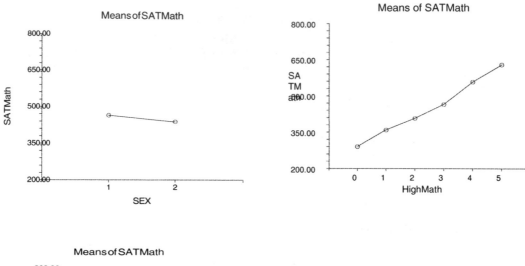

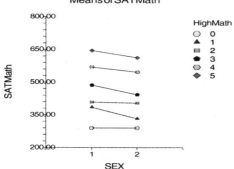

Fisher's LSD Multiple-Comparison Test

Response: SATMath
Term B: HighMath
Alpha = 0.050 Error Term = S(AB) DF = 212 MSE = 6253.718 Critical Value = 1.959964

Group	Count	Mean	Different From Groups
0	5	290	2, 3, 4, 5
1	17	358.8333	2, 3, 4, 5
2	80	406.2822	0, 1, 3, 4, 5
3	61	464.4318	0, 1, 2, 4, 5
4	35	557.8497	0, 1, 2, 3, 5
5	26	628.619	0, 1, 2, 3, 4

Alpha = 0.050 Error Term = S(AB) DF = 212 MSE = 6253.718

Fisher's LSD Multiple-Comparison Test

Response: SATMath
Term AB: SEX,HighMath
Alpha = 0.050 Error Term = S(AB) DF = 212 MSE = 6253.718 Critical Value = 1.959964

Different Group	Count	Mean	From Groups
2,0	3	290	(2,2), (1,2), (2,3), (1,3), (2,4), (1,4) (2,5), (1,5)
1,0	2	290	(2,2), (1,2), (2,3), (1,3), (2,4), (1,4) (2,5), (1,5)
2,1	15	332.6667	(2,2), (1,2), (2,3), (1,3), (2,4), (1,4) (2,5), (1,5)
1,1	2	385	(2,4), (1,4), (2,5), (1,5)
2,2	43	404.186	(2,0), (1,0), (2,1), (2,3), (1,3), (2,4) (1,4), (2,5), (1,5)
1,2	37	408.3784	(2,0), (1,0), (2,1), (1,3), (2,4), (1,4) (2,5), (1,5)
2,3	28	442.5	(2,0), (1,0), (2,1), (2,2), (1,3), (2,4) (1,4), (2,5), (1,5)
1,3	33	486.3636	(2,0), (1,0), (2,1), (2,2), (1,2), (2,3) (2,4), (1,4), (2,5), (1,5)
2,4	13	546.1539	(2,0), (1,0), (2,1), (1,1), (2,2), (1,2) (2,3), (1,3), (1,5)
1,4	22	569.5455	(2,0), (1,0), (2,1), (1,1), (2,2), (1,2) (2,3), (1,3), (1,5)
2,5	5	612	(2,0), (1,0), (2,1), (1,1), (2,2), (1,2) (2,3), (1,3)
1,5	21	645.2381	(2,0), (1,0), (2,1), (1,1), (2,2), (1,2) (2,3), (1,3), (2,4), (1,4)

ANCOVA: SATMath, GPA, SEX, HighMath

Analysis of Variance Table

Source Term	DF	Sum of Squares	Mean Square	F-Ratio	Prob Level	Power (Alpha = 0.05)
X(GPA)	1	60742.07	60742.07	10.13	0.001678*	0.870702
A: SEX	1	14469.19	14469.19	2.41	0.121803	0.325902
B: HighMath	5	619111.7	123822.3	20.65	0.000000*	1.000000
AB	5	19151.22	3830.244	0.64	0.670291	0.223343
S	211	1265046	5995.479			
Total (Adjusted)	223	3177384				
Total	224					

* Term significant at alpha = 0.05

Means and Standard Error Section

Term	Count	Mean	Standard Error
All	224	454.7165	
A: SEX			
1	117	468.4878	7.15845
2	107	440.9452	7.485487
B: HighMath			
0	5	320.5056	34.62796
1	17	378.3761	18.77965
2	80	415.3408	8.656991
3	61	462.4599	9.913957
4	35	545.8635	13.08814
5	26	605.7529	15.18537
AB: SEX,HighMath			
1,0	2	320.074	54.75162
1,1	2	405.147	54.75162
1,2	37	421.3746	12.72949
1,3	33	490.0963	13.47892
1,4	22	554.9085	16.50823
1,5	21	619.326	16.89672
2,0	3	320.9373	44.70451
2,1	15	351.6051	19.99246
2,2	43	409.3069	11.80804
2,3	28	434.8235	14.63299
2,4	13	536.8185	21.47535
2,5	5	592.1798	34.62796

Plots Section

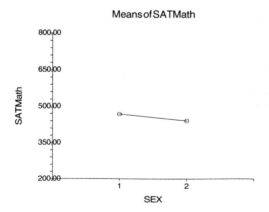

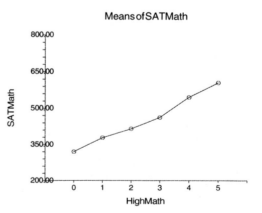

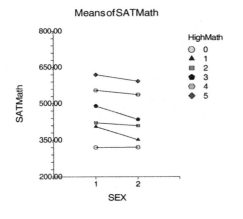

Means of SATMath

Fisher's LSD Multiple-Comparison Test
Response: SATMath
Term B: HighMath
Alpha = 0.050 Error Term = S(AB) DF = 211 MSE = 5995.479 Critical Value = 1.959964

Group	Count	Mean	Different From Groups
0	5	320.5056	2, 3, 4, 5
1	17	378.3761	3, 4, 5
2	80	415.3408	0, 3, 4, 5
3	61	462.4599	0, 1, 2, 4, 5
4	35	545.8635	0, 1, 2, 3, 5
5	26	605.7529	0, 1, 2, 3, 4

WARNING:
The standard errors of the means do not include
Fisher's LSD Multiple-Comparison Test
Response: SATMath
Term AB: SEX,HighMath
Alpha = 0.050 Error Term = S(AB) DF = 211 MSE = 5995.479 Critical Value = 1.959964

Group	Count	Mean	Different From Groups
1,0	2	320.074	(2,3), (1,3), (2,4), (1,4), (2,5), (1,5)
2,0	3	320.9373	(1,2), (2,3), (1,3), (2,4), (1,4), (2,5) (1,5)
2,1	15	351.6051	(2,2), (1,2), (2,3), (1,3), (2,4), (1,4) (2,5), (1,5)
1,1	2	405.147	(2,4), (1,4), (2,5), (1,5)
2,2	43	409.3069	(2,1), (1,3), (2,4), (1,4), (2,5), (1,5)
1,2	37	421.3746	(2,0), (2,1), (1,3), (2,4), (1,4), (2,5) (1,5)
2,3	28	434.8235	(1,0), (2,0), (2,1), (1,3), (2,4), (1,4) (2,5), (1,5)

Group	Count	Mean	From Groups
1,3	33	490.0963	(1,0), (2,0), (2,1), (2,2), (1,2), (2,3) (1,4), (2,5), (1,5)
2,4	13	536.8185	(1,0), (2,0), (2,1), (1,1), (2,2), (1,2) (2,3), (1,5)
1,4	22	554.9085	(1,0), (2,0), (2,1), (1,1), (2,2), (1,2) (2,3), (1,3), (1,5)
2,5	5	592.1798	(1,0), (2,0), (2,1), (1,1), (2,2), (1,2) (2,3), (1,3)
1,5	21	619.326	(1,0), (2,0), (2,1), (1,1), (2,2), (1,2) (2,3), (1,3), (2,4), (1,4)

WARNING:

The standard errors of the means do not include

an allowance for the sampling error of the covariate(s).

Hence, any post-hoc tests based on these results are to be considered conservative.

APPENDIX F

ENGSCO DATABASE

ENGSCO DATABASE DESCRIPTION
This data base consists of the following elements and was fictionally created:

1.   Analysis unit: a college freshman
2.   Sample: AUs from a large freshman class.
3.   Sample size: 45
4.   Characteristics:
        4.1   **Freshmks**:   freshman final English mark (column 1)
        4.2   **CAT**:   a version of aptitude test score (column 2)
        4.3   **HS_GPA**:   high school grade point average (column 3)
        4.4   **ENG_PRE**:   a freshman English pre-test score, scaled from 0–50 (column 4)

Row	FRESHMKS	CAT	HS_GPA	ENG_PRE
1	76	132	3	21.0
2	92	147	4	40.0
3	68	67	2	14.0
4	60	128	2	18.0
5	76	103	3	26.0
6	88	108	2	13.0
7	72	101	3	20.0
8	88	125	3	28.0
9	96	129	4	30.0
10	96	127	3	15.0
11	64	93	1	15.0
12	96	142	3	39.0
13	88	113	3	15.0
14	40	93	2	8.0
15	96	105	3	20.0
16	52	99	3	13.0
17	68	124	2	27.0
18	68	105	3	25.0
19	44	144	2	20.0
20	92	106	3	22.0
21	52	100	3	22.0
22	80	98	3	13.0
23	52	83	2	21.0
24	92	99	3	31.0
25	76	107	2	13.0
26	92	131	3	29.0

Row	FRESHMKS	CAT	HS_GPA	ENG_PRE
27	76	98	3	20.0
28	88	117	3	33.0
29	88	156	4	26.0
30	88	117	3	25.0
31	96	105	3	34.0
32	72	108	3	21.0
33	64	94	3	8.0
34	96	152	4	43.0
35	48	115	2	12.0
36	76	132	3	15.0
37	88	90	4	24.0
38	88	104	3	24.0
39	84	129	3	18.0
40	88	102	3	12.0
41	48	98	2	20.0
42	80	124	2	21.0
43	96	121	4	37.0
44	92	129	3	23.0
45	64	104	2	18.0

CORRELATION MATRIX

	FRESHMKS	CAT	HS_GPA	ENG_PRE
FRESHMKS	1.000000	0.365899	0.669243	0.544108
CAT	0.365899	1.000000	0.432899	0.505623
HS_GPA	0.669243	0.432899	1.000000	0.526978
ENG_PRE	0.544108	0.505623	0.526978	1.000000

Cronbachs Alpha = 0.595427 Standardized Cronbachs Alpha = 0.804731

BIVARIATE REGRESSION REPORT (TWO VARIABLES)

Independent Variable	Regression Coefficient	Standard Error	T-Value (Ho: B = 0)	Prob Level	Decision (5%)	Power (5%)
Intercept	21.59244	9.630899	2.2420	0.030174	Reject Ho	0.591660
HS_GPA	20.01386	3.388655	5.9061	0.000001	Reject Ho	0.999931
R-Squared	0.447886					

MULTIPLE REGRESSION REPORT (THREE VARIABLES)

Independent Variable	Regression Coefficient	Standard Error	T-Value (Ho: B = 0)	Prob Level	Decision (5%)	Power (5%)
Intercept	21.80332	9.286905	2.3477	0.023673	Reject Ho	0.630767
HS_GPA	15.8371	3.844573	4.1193	0.000174	Reject Ho	0.980467
ENG_PRE	0.5189717	0.251735	2.0616	0.045472	Reject Ho	0.521713
R-Squared	0.498622					

MULTIPLE REGRESSION REPORT (FOUR VARIABLES)

Independent Variable	Regression Coefficient	Standard Error	T-Value (Ho: B = 0)	Prob Level	Decision (5%)
INTERCEPT	21.56957	12.4945	1.7263	0.091818	Accept Ho
CAT	3.240711E–03	0.1141271	0.0284	0.977484	Accept Ho
HS_GPA	15.81134	3.995442	3.9573	0.000294	Reject Ho
ENG_PRE	0.5161603	0.273345	1.8883	0.066074	Accept Ho

R-Squared	0.498632

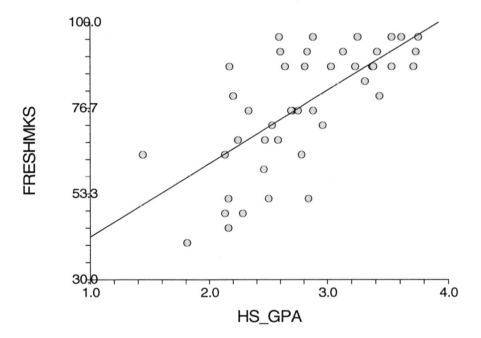

HS_GPAvsFRESHMKS

INDEX

1-58348-841-3

Printed in the United States
98659LV00006B/20/A